Breaking Free

Lose the illusionary self, find

S erenity
E nergy
L ove
F low

Christian M. Wiese

BALBOA.PRESS
A DIVISION OF HAY HOUSE

Balboa Press books may be ordered through booksellers or by contacting:

Balboa Press
A Division of Hay House
1663 Liberty Drive
Bloomington, IN 47403
www.balboapress.com
844-682-1282

Because of the dynamic nature of the Internet, any web addresses or
links contained in this book may have changed since publication and
may no longer be valid. The views expressed in this work are solely those
of the author and do not necessarily reflect the views of the publisher,
and the publisher hereby disclaims any responsibility for them.

Any people depicted in stock imagery provided by Getty Images are
models, and such images are being used for illustrative purposes only.
Certain stock imagery © Getty Images.

Print information available on the last page.

ISBN: 979-8-7652-2524-0 (sc)
ISBN: 979-8-7652-2526-4 (hc)
ISBN: 979-8-7652-2525-7 (e)

Library of Congress Control Number: 2022903150

Balboa Press rev. date: 04/04/2022

To my soul family—you know who you are!

We are all going to the same place, and we are all on a path. Sometimes our paths converge. Sometimes they separate, and we can hardly see each other, much less hear each other. But on the good days, we're walking on the same path, close together, and we are walking each other Home.

Ram Dass

CONTENTS

GLIMPSES OF S-E-L-F

INTRODUCTION

Lead me from dreaming to waking.
Lead me from opacity to clarity.
Lead me from the complicated to the simple.
Lead me from the obscure to the obvious.
Lead me from intention to attention.
Lead me from what I'm told I am to what I see
I am.
Lead me from confrontation to wide openness.
Lead me to the Place I never left,
where there is peace.

The Upanishads

I was talking to a friend from the UK on the phone. I forget what exactly we were talking about at the time but all of a sudden she asked me, "What are you feeling right now?" Surprised, I responded, "What do you mean?" Nothing came to mind. I was focused on our conversation instead. She said, "Well, let me tell you what I am feeling. I feel pressure in the back of the head. I feel energy in the neck. I feel tension in the right thigh." Wow, that was surprising. There was in fact an energy running through my head. There also was that bubbly feeling in the neck area that I so often experience. I was also sitting cross-legged, so there was indeed pressure on my right thigh! It was only when she mentioned it that I became aware of these sensations.

How can we account for these phenomena? How can someone sitting 3,000 miles away without any visual contact tell her counterpart how his body feels? It's quite simple actually. We are One! We all have access to these metaphysical perceptions like my friend from the UK did during our conversation. Anyone who tunes into the prevailing Oneness can have metaphysical experiences like that. Anyone who awakens from our narrow self-identification, from our mundane existence of competition, egoism and robotic nature, can do so, and the amazing world of

S erenity
E nergy
L ove
F low

awaits. Our S-E-L-F is always where our illusionary s-e-l-f— selfishness, envy, loneliness, frustration, to name just a few attributions of the misplaced "me, myself and I" identification— ceases to be. I proved that to myself while working in a fairly competitive and stressful workplace and experienced a magical ride over a time span of ten years. I lived my spiritual truths while reaching new professional heights at the same time. If we can experience S-E-L-F in such an environment, it should be possible to accomplish this feat in all areas of our lives. I believe that everyone who signs up for an awakening journey can get to that stage. A spiritual quest has some very concrete and mind-blowing perks.

Can we consciously break free from our self though? Can we jump over our own shadow? Not really but we can slip into a higher dimension of being where this illusionary self ceases to be. We can awaken from our illusionary self! Actually, it's the other way around, our spiritual being is the natural state and we can always return to it. We can—momentarily at least—step out of our own agenda, the fears, and the many inner drives. We can leave behind what we are not, the conditioning and the painful past we carry around. We can step out of an energy field of "me, myself and I", and once we do, a new world opens up. We can do that here and now in the magnificence of the moment and in the stillness of our being. On the outside, our self-identification takes a step back when we stumble on a new world of seemingly magical connections. Our overactive minds are wowed into silence and the fears and agendas suddenly lose all importance because what we see and experience is way too fascinating to put our own personal spin on it. On the inside, our vibrations increase naturally when we get still. This increase of our heart-center vibrations is part of the expanding kundalini energy that we will discuss in this book. "Breaking Free" aims to reconnect you with this higher dimension of being, at home, at work, in the silence of your own being; everywhere really.

"I Am That I Am" manifests differently for all of us but serenity, love and mind-blowing metaphysical experiences are all hallmarks of the blissful state. My friend from the UK experienced a unitive state when she talked to me on the phone that day. She was as much in touch with my body as she was with hers, 3000 miles apart. People tuned in spiritually have these metaphysical experiences all the time and this book will share many examples of the group of friends I have interviewed. Moments when we experience Oneness are countless and they happen to all of us. Maybe you have experienced an aha moment when you suddenly understand your own agenda and sidestepped it because that's what the here and now invited you to do. Then, amazingly, even without an agenda the end result of the interaction with others turned out to be extremely fulfilling, and more so than your little self could ever have surmised. That's the state of Grace that is always available to all of us.

We awaken from our illusionary self on the inside when we are connected to our heart energy. We are S-E-L-F on the outside when life simply flows through us. Just like a prism, we channel the light without being in the way but coloring the environment with our authentic presence, our true color so to speak. Every person has a unique energy signature and a big part of the spiritual quest is to create our little garden of fulfillment, love and serenity that allows us to be who we are. Initially we try to create that garden consciously and life tends to interfere with our plans occasionally, but soon we realize that life creates this garden for us. All we have to do is to show up and, well, be!

Everyone who starts asking spiritual questions is invited to join. My awakening started in 2008 and I observe happily that many more newcomers are joining these days. Everyone is called to join and all it takes is a shift in perspective and the higher dimension of being is ready to rush to our side. I used to have an elitist mindset and figured that some of us are simply born to experience this awakening experience, but a client showed me that everyone who asks spiritual questions is called to join this higher dimension of being. He requested a couple of chats to better understand the spiritual world his partner lived in.

Yet, the moment he started asking his own questions, a new world appeared to him as well. On a trip to Germany—to my hometown of all places, in Berlin—he experienced incredible synchronicities. He was riding exactly the same ascension wave that I had enjoyed in 2008. Everyone is called, and the moment you start asking for guidance, it opens up.

"Breaking Free" also is the third book in a series that aims to provide an ascension manual for spiritual newcomers who are embarking on a quest of leaving the illusionary self behind. My first book, "The Magnificent Experiment" shares the excitement when a new world beyond my wildest imagination opened up to me. Its sequel, "The Way of the Meister" offers a bit more seasoned perspective and aims to help the reader integrate the newly found world with the old one. This book is the boldest of the three, claiming that leaving this twilight zone of bipolar existence is just a step away. "Breaking Free" also provides a new feature to make this book more relevant for your specific awakening quest. Our experience of this awakening is bound to differ so besides reflecting on my own breaking free observations, I also reached out to 41 long standing spiritual friends and asked them to share their journeys. Our combined insights should provide many of the answers that you are looking for. We may be all on idiosyncratic paths but we all reach the same destination in the end.

Are you ready to break free?

THE DAWN

Awareness is a constant process of liberation.
J. Krishnamurti

MINDING THE ILLUSIONARY SELF

Many of our thoughts and actions that we think reflect our self are not what they seem. We believe we have freedom to choose, but, in many instances, the choices occur in the absence of any deliberation and often under the influence of others.
The Self-Illusion: How the Social Brain
Creates Identity by Bruce Hood

My mother has been investing in the stock market for the last 50 years. Mostly she hasn't done so well but the hope to do better next year keeps her going. Investing in the stock market is her hobby just like some enjoy playing chess or buying lottery tickets. When I was younger, she talked endlessly about John Maynard Keynes, the world-famous economist. At one point, she also wanted to write a book. She unfortunately didn't make it past a few pages and added, "Writing a book is really hard". Now let me see, I got a PhD in economics and spent a couple of decades analyzing financial markets and you are now holding my third book in your hands. The question arises, am I merely living my mother's aspirations? Are we all just puppets, acting out the wants and fears of our upbringings and surroundings while we claim that we are in charge? Spirituality argues what some neurological scientists also echo, our perceived self is illusionary. Yes, we are conditioned and manipulated marionettes but we have the power to step out of it. With awakening we are catapulted in a completely different dimension. I am living proof of this. Today I am a spiritual writer and coach and no one in my family has anything to do with this calling. Religion and spirituality was never a big deal in our household.

We can break free from our conditioning when a mysterious dimension beyond our little "I"-identity makes contact and takes over the steering wheel. We can step out of our self in the here and now. Science and spirituality agree that our self is illusionary. We take our self as our real identity even though it is a bundle of feelings, thoughts and sensations wrapped up in a convenient story that changes all the time. Countless psychological experiments and neurological revelations have shown that "the story of me" has giant holes in it. Many memories are mostly made around times when we felt something intensely. We are conditioned by our upbringing—as I likely was by my mother's passions. We are primed by our environment, often without realizing it. The scientist argues that we have to work with what we have and offers some psychological and neurological insights to cover our blind spots. Spirituality, just like psychology, encourages us to heal and to integrate all aspects of our being and become whole. What is different though is that with awakening a higher dimension opens up to us that transcends "the story of me" altogether. We manage to step out of that illusionary self-image and learn to be powered by our heart energy and grasp that we are not our mind, body, or life experience. The acronym S-E-L-F, Serenity, Energy, Love, Flow, attempts to put this unitive experience in words. Oneness, Awareness, Consciousness, "I Am That I Am", and Grace are some other expressions that you will encounter throughout the book to articulate the indescribable. Consistent with my prior books, I use capital letters to describe these states that our illusionary self seemingly cannot reach.

"I Am That I Am" is always in plain sight, it is us who are too distracted to take notice. Yet, we can develop the spiritual eye to perceive Oneness in life's confusing dualities. We connect with our loving heart what is perceived as the energy of people and places. We open up to Consciousness, the downloaded insights from a higher dimension of being. And we can participate in the flow of life that uses us as a mere conductor.

Awakening is a state that kicks in one day, just as pregnancy is the beginning of a new life within a mother. At least that was my experience when I was in my early 40s. It felt like a new birth of sorts. Reading through the survey responses of my friends that I gathered for this book, I also encountered a different perspective. Several participants claimed that we are born free and just temporarily forget who we are. They vividly remembered the feeling that they felt trapped in an alien body in early childhood. So, the message instead becomes that we are born free, but that we are called to absorb and digest the genetic, parental and societal influences that are superimposed on us until we can eventually reclaim our true divine origin. As one participant put it, "It started in my childhood when I was about 3 or 4. I was standing under the kitchen table thinking, "What am I doing in this body?" She knew that she was born free.

It's an exhilarating life that awaits us when we drop the dictate of our illusionary self identification. Life becomes full of synchronicity, serenity, joy, laughter, meaningful connections and love to an extent that we never quite experienced with such intensity before. At the same time though, this journey has its confusing moments as well. The superimposed world that we are born into is persistent indeed and has a habit of getting the better of us. We look down on the stuff that bubbles to the surface from the depth of our being and we judge it as the interference that stands between us and freedom, not knowing that we only judge our self. So, we end up being caught in two different worlds, unable to whole-heartedly commit to either. Frustrated we ask, is there a way to break free?

The pull of millions of years of evolution is not easy to let go of. So, let's accept that we are in a twilight zone for a while and make the most of this experience. A little effort is needed to make the commitment to the new world complete. A clear vision is required to sign up for the right professional calling and to hang out with the folks we truly resonate with. The message of this book though is that in all the necessary transforming, healing, letting go of the past, and repositioning towards living a more authentic, passionate and purposeful life we should not lose sight of the fact that a higher state of being is always present, ready to connect whenever we are. Engulfed in the illusionary self we want to break free, yet viewed from this higher state of being we are already free, here and now. That's the paradox we try to get our arms around in this book. A world beyond our little perceived self is always but a step away. Let's discover it together!

A GLIMPSE OF ONENESS

It was a vacation day in 1999. My friend went on a hike with his son. Suddenly something extraordinary happened. The sky seemed to open up and time stood still. All his movements up a steep climb were effortless. His backpack had no weight whatsoever. The color of the grass, the plants, the sky and even the rocks seemed more vivid. He had read the descriptions of the flow state by some top athletes and surgeons, and this moment seemed to be this flow experience magnified 100 times. He had never taken drugs but he doubted that any of these psychedelic spectacles could come anywhere close. I asked him how long this satori experience was and he answered that the most exuberant phase lasted 5-10 minutes, though the effect could be felt the entire day.

I have experienced these satori moments when time seemingly stands still as well. You probably have too. I started my first book, "The Magnificent Experiment", with a description of the most surreal experience I had in a conference room filled with economists and financial experts discussing the end of the world as we know it at the onset of the global financial crisis in 2008. I felt energy rising within me and my thoughts stopped completely. For 10-20 minutes, I felt I was finally Home! While this intense feeling of wholeness and peace passed afterwards, it was that day when I realized for good that something in me had changed. My friend who shared his satori moment on the hiking trail with his son is just one of the amazing survey responses that I received. These spiritual breakthroughs happened everywhere; at work, in periods of serious distress and in joyful encounters with loved ones, even while giving birth in one survey response. Awakening finds us wherever we are. Life triggers breakthrough experiences for us when we are ready to receive them and often it takes very little to push us over the metaphysical edge.

We are tempted to chase these spiritual experiences but they come when they come. We can't force anything and instead we are encouraged to work on what is holding us back. We learn to become mindful of the self identification at work. Spiritual living is essentially the preparation in the more mundane states for the next "cessation of self" experience. We are invited to do some healing and mindful reflection in the meantime. You might say, Awareness is present all the time, but in the moments when our conditioning takes over we can at least practice self-awareness.

We are transformed along life's journey and enjoy the magic as it comes. When I reflect back on these unitive experiences, nothing has really changed in these 12 years of awakening. The magic moments of serenity, synchronicity, love and connectedness feel as mind blowing today as they did then. However, what has changed is that I no longer look for anything. I live my life day in, day out, knowing that I am guided by something greater than myself. The two worlds that competed for my attention over many years have become one, a steady invite to connect with what lies beyond self here and now. I claim that everyone can get to this stage. In hindsight, this stage of spiritual living is really not a big deal, even though it seems like such a big deal when you are hunting for it. I figure there are many who live these perennial truths without feeling the need to talk about it. From the outside, they seem as normal as they come, though everyone who spends time with them feels a magnetic pull of love and serenity emanating from them.

There are concrete steps everyone can take who wants to be part of this serene empowered, loving and unitive state of being, and this book aims to provide you with some inspirations and different approaches that you can try out as well. We can be present when our mind speculates about the future, or when the pain body of prior traumas triggers another self-inflicted demolition course. We can heal and let go of these pain bodies, allowing us to travel lighter. We can reconnect with our passion and life purpose, making our life joyful and meaningful again. We can surround ourselves with serene energy, the people we love, the places and activities that allow our authentic self to shine through.

There is no hierarchy when it comes to spirituality. It is just that not everyone has opened up to the invite from what lies beyond yet because some of us are still too busy working on whatever our heart and mind is set on. This is absolutely okay and often the most spiritual contribution to the soul development of this person. We have no business judging and comparing anyone and have to remember that the breakthrough to the next dimension of being can happen to anyone at any time. Often the breakthrough is at hand when we don't like what we have created for ourselves. It is then that we open up and look for a new way. You can never say who is next in the awakening—one glimpse at what lies beyond self and there is no turning back.

SYNCHRONICITY–JUST ENJOY THE RIDE

Synchronicity is an ever-present reality for those who have eyes to see.

Carl Jung

We often hear spiritual travelers inquiring about beautiful number sequences, or other meaningful occurrences that are just too frequent to be considered random. So, they naturally ask what this is all about. My response to this question is that synchronicity is an initiation of sorts. The Beyond is making contact with us and we are invited to learn a new language. Numbers are captured by the "science" of numerology. Animals, objects, and people are interpreted by psychologists and shamans. Spiritual phenomena are perceived and experienced by our different faiths, and so forth. In short, an amazing spiritual quest is about to launch for everyone who wants to engage. A crash course in making this unitive experience a permanent reality, "Enjoy the ride!", is perhaps the best advice we can give when someone is embarking on an awakening journey.

Two questions come to mind when synchronicity first pops up, "How does this happen?" and "What exactly do we do with it?" The answer to the how is simple. It is hard for our mind to grasp that beyond the world that we are living in is a world of Oneness that is patiently waiting for us to connect.

This Beyond will never interfere with our belief system. While we live in the world that our logical minds and deepest fears expect to encounter, we are trapped like the sleepers in the movie "The Matrix". Yet, our situation is not as dismal as the movie makes it appear. Many of us have awoken to our true nature; the enlightened folks, the poets and some artists as well. Everyone can in fact. That's the message of synchronicity and serendipity. That's what the beautiful strings of numbers, meaningful coincidences and other Spirit messages are about. We receive a wink from the Beyond to take another look at what is truly going on. Especially mind-driven, left-brain folks likes me are susceptible to synchronicity. Our artists, nature lovers and devoted spiritual travelers have other modes of perception and don't need numbers to see that we are One. Synchronicity is an initiation but there is so much more to follow. With a spiritual eye to see and a loving heart to feel we are introduced to what lies beyond the self. Be open for mind-blowing experiences but don't start reading meaning into randomness in your quest to be spiritual either. Our mind loves synchronicity and encrypted messages, so by running after synchronicity we may invent yet another roadblock on the journey to leave the mind behind.

The answer to the second question, what exactly should we do with it, is entirely up to us. I remember when my spiritual path opened up, I received spiritual and real-life messages in the form of song lyrics on the radio and Massachusetts license plates. I was naturally inclined to use them. Getting information a little before other folks do, using meaningful connections for professional purpose, and so forth. I had fun with synchronicity and had a decent track record using this information. Eventually though I moved on from it. I realized that these signs are not that helpful on a journey to leave the mind behind. These days I rarely look for anything, so my mind has little to hold on to. Sometimes I still get a little energy boost when I see a meaningful wink from the Beyond, and I am naturally grateful. Grace is always right where we are.

James Redfield made synchronicity popular in the spiritual community with his bestseller, "The Celestine Prophecy". In it, the synchronicity concept became so much more than just meaningful number sequences or serendipitous encounters. His book argued that in its limit, the law of synchronicity says that every interaction, every conversation or event is the Beyond making a connection with us. That's how I live my life these days. I welcome everything that life confronts me with, the supposedly "good" as well as the apparent "bad". As the 13th century Sufi mystic Rumi put it, "If everyone is God speaking, why not be polite and listen?"

The German quantum physicist Werner Heisenberg once said,

"The first gulp from the glass of natural science will turn you into an atheist, but at the bottom God is waiting for you."

That is it really! We get initiated with a specific talent or a vision of Oneness and we spend a lifetime to make the jump to the new world complete. Many paths lead to Rome they say, or in our case, Home. Learn the new language, get yourself out of the way as best as you can and always show your true colors. Whenever spiritual newcomers ask about synchronicity, kundalini awakening, twin flames or "dark night of the soul" episodes, I send them notes like this chapter to help them with their journey. The most important reminder though is that a Force beyond our wildest imagination has just made contact that will take care of everything. So, the best piece of advice we can give is, "Just enjoy the ride!"

AWARENESS–IN SEARCH OF THE BLUE SKY

In Awareness there is no becoming, there is no end to be gained. There is silent observation without choice and condemnation, from which there comes understanding.

J. Krishnamurti

Awareness is hard to describe. It's not thinking, though thoughts pop to the surface as an afterthought. It's not feeling either, though serene and blissful feelings are a part of it. It's a silent observation, as J. Krishnamurti puts it well. It's an understanding that we are embedded in something that is beyond us, while being an essential part of it as well. For lack of a better expression, it's the here and now, the moment worth living for. I picture Awareness as the blue sky. It is always there, but sometimes clouds move in, or showers. We do our daily stuff, we get caught up in our affairs but deep down inside many of us know that the sun is shining up there. Some people are too busy to notice the magic of the here and now. Some are too busy blaming the past or too involved scheming for the future. Some want sex, success, or fortune. Some want revenge, some want power, and many want to escape from an inner void. We all have these unconscious moments but with awakening also comes the ability to snap out of it and return to the center of our being quicker than before. Awareness never leaves. There are just some clouds that temporarily block the blazing sun.

According to Google, there are 266 days of sunshine in San Diego and 166 days in Cleveland Ohio. So, when my clients tell me that it is blue sky that they are after, I ask them why they aren't moving south. There are concrete steps we can take to open up to Awareness. There are many self-imposed interferences that we can cut out to open up to the here and now. "Breaking Free" aims to provide a roadmap of how to live a more sun-filled life. It will give you glimpses of freedom, but the ultimate enlightened state is to be equally happy living in Cleveland as in San Diego, to have that cessation of self, independent of whether you are lying in the sun or dancing in the rain.

One theme we will return to over and over in this book is that we can strive for the transformation of self, just as much as having the ability to drop our illusionary self-identification in the present moment. The process of self-transformation and the feat of stepping out of the self-identification are two different perspectives. A surfer may be happier in San Diego and it may take him time to relocate to Southern California. That's the transformation at work; a more meaningful job, a deeper connection with our friends and lover. Yet, the connection with the higher dimension brings happiness and fulfillment here and now independent of circumstances and location. Yes, there is a process to awakening—a transformation, a healing, a letting go, an expressing of our authentic self—that we can work on and that life confronts us with. We get happier over time and more fulfilled once we get to know our authentic self better and manage to express it. Yet, in all the healing, transforming, problem solving and becoming more authentic we shouldn't overlook that the invite for the next unitive state is always here and now.

I am a spiritual life coach and I can help you with your transformation. Some need to empower themselves. Some need to face their demons. Some need to forgive others and themselves. Many have a healing journey and a soul-searching quest ahead. I might be able to boost the experienced sunshine to 266 days in the year up from 166 by encouraging you to make the change you thus far haven't been able to. I suffered panic attacks in earlier years when the stress of my work got to me. Some of my friends battled addictions, and all of us have lost loved ones. Pain is what started the spiritual quest in many of us. As it turns out, rain is as needed for our spiritual harvest just as much as sunshine. Unfortunately, sometimes it is the thunderstorms that break us open. If you remember "It never rains in Southern California" song, you may also remember this part that is somewhat hidden in the pleasant tune:

> *Seems it never rains in southern California*
> *Seems I've often heard that kind of talk before*
> *It never rains in California, but girl, don't they warn ya?*
> *It pours, man, it pours.*
>
> It never rains in Southern California; Songwriters, Albert Hammond / Mike Hazlewood

When it rains, it pours! Freedom requires complete surrender. So, in order to proceed to the blue sky paradigm, we sometimes have to accept the deluge as well. We see the vortex coming at us. We shake in our boots full of fear but jump into it because there is no other choice. That's what it means to be free. Freedom is only found in the vortex when we have let go of all the remaining efforts of clinging, avoiding and scheming. Life is designed to take everyone Home anyway and it happens rain or shine. Everyone is on a subconscious quest towards freedom, but it is only after awakening that this letting go process becomes visible to us. The spiritual life coach helps bringing in a little more sunshine into your life. Yet, it's the inner revolution that delivers the Light, and only Grace can accomplish this feat. For the moment, keep an eye on the process as well as the now until the revolution is complete. That's what I and many of my friends did and it worked quite well. That way, every moment is spiritual, whether you feel it or not. Every moment is an opportunity to enjoy Awareness, or to be simply self-aware when the old programs of the past have gotten the better of us once again.

In the state of Awareness, we dance in the rain just as we enjoy the sunshine. In contrast, self-awareness is like sitting at home when the rain sets in, knowing that we are being prepared for the next harvest. In a spiritual quest, every moment is welcome.

SERENITY—A BOON ON THE BASEBALL FIELD

There is no "you"; there is only the state of freedom. Be That. Be free like the sky. Be still like the hill. Accept change like the seasons. Be silent like complete emptiness. You are That!

Ramana Maharshi

It was a beautiful summer day in Massachusetts. I was out on the field watching the boys play baseball. The boys had fun and it could have been a perfect moment in time but there was a longing in me, an inner restlessness, that kept me from enjoying it. I texted my spiritual friend, "I just want to have that peace of mind that I once felt". Her response came back, "You will find it!" The truth of her promise was ringing in my ears. The scenery was picture perfect and I felt God's presence granting me that boon at that moment. A little work would still be ahead to claim it though. There would still be a few sleepless nights and a couple of panic attacks when financial markets were once again getting the better of me. Then one day, magically, serenity filled me and this feeling of freedom has stayed with me. A transformation from fear to serenity is a perk of awakening. Everyone can claim it!

At the time of writing this book, financial markets were crashing again due to the pandemic fear of the Corona virus. I was reminded of the existential fear I sometimes experienced when I used to work in the financial industry. Around that time when markets were turning against me at work, I felt panic. I was nauseous. More than once the temptation crossed my mind to simply jump off a bridge to make that pain go away. All that seems so childish in hindsight. Who suffered panic? I was the "I"-identification that just hated to be caught on the wrong side of the trade. Today I am convinced that I have to thank the pressure of my old job for cracking something inside of me open which launched me on a quest for the kind of freedom Ramana Maharshi describes in the above quote. The amazing thing is, you don't even need to wait for the good times to roll in. You can have the "cessation of self" moment occurring all the time, even when the going gets tough.

Existential fear is more pressing than dealing with the "me energy" when the going is supposedly good. You scream out in despair, "there's got to be a better way!", and sometimes, that's exactly when a higher dimension opens up to us. In contrast, in the so-called "good times", there is still a little apathy, a little loneliness, some restlessness or boredom. We pretend that isn't us and we just sweep these little cravings and irritations under the carpet. We escape from the inner void rather than facing it. Be alert, truthful and vigilant in all situations and never mind the perceived bad times either. Policy makers during the many financial crises tended to say, "Don't let a good crisis go to waste", implying that they now could finally push through the unpopular reforms since everyone could see that there was no alternative. A spiritual quest is different from policy making though. Your mind is probably saying right now, "Yes, I want to make that change I always wanted to do", and sure, absolutely, go for it. We have a little spiritual homework to do if we want to get anywhere. Yet, when I say, "Don't let a good crisis go to waste", I mean something a lot more revolutionary than making a change. No matter what change you are implementing, your "me energy" will still be running the show. I am encouraging you to use the crack that broke open in this crisis and look straight into the incoming Light. The world that Ramana Maharshi is describing is always at our disposal. It is the "you" that disappears in the here and now.

There are many ways of reaching this freedom Ramana Maharshi describes in the above quote and probably as many paths as there are people on planet earth. I am a mind driven person so I was naturally attracted to knowing, the study of the spiritual intellect. I started seeing spiritual messages and wisdom in life itself. Some of my friends focus more on the fun ride of the journey. Butterfly like, they jump from flower to flower in the spur of the moment, following the energy of the flow and enjoying it. The Buddhists in our community zoom into the stillness of the moment instead, while the Christians are after unconditional love. All paths get us to our destination and over the years I have traveled most of them. What is most important though is that you find the path that works best for you. We all get to the same destination in the end when our self is entirely absent, and when the "me energy" returns, we all have our own notion of spiritual living and our method to re-center to the core of our being once again. There are no shortcuts to freedom. There is only your approach of opening up what lies beyond self. Discover what approach works for you.

Reflect a moment and tell me which part of the higher dimension in the S-E-L-F acronym is most meaningful to you—peace of mind, abundant energy flow, love or an empowering participation in the flow of life:

S erenity
E nergy
L ove
F low

Say a prayer and make a wish—it has already been granted like it was given to me years back. Sure, it takes a few years to raise our vibrations and manifest the professional outlet that allows us to shine, to attract our soul partner and tribe that vibe with us, but that's part of the breaking free process too. The transformation is complete when creating, manifesting and attracting becomes part of being. Are you ready to claim your boon?

THE DAY-MAKER

Your way then will be one continuous round of blessing. Wherever you go will My Light shine and My Love radiate forth about you, creating Peace, Concord, Unity. The great thing will be that everyone will be better and happier by reason of your appearance in their lives.

Joseph Brenner

A hairstylist flew business class when a stern looking fellow traveler asked him what he did professionally. Instead of being intimidated he answered instinctively, "Day Maker". The gentleman who had asked the question was confused about this answer and wanted to know what that was exactly. The hairstylist responded that an important function of his job was to make a person's day. Afterwards he was so proud of his newly minted title that he even put it on his business card.

Years later a woman came into his shop. She was a regular customer but she came in between her appointments so he figured that she must have had an important event to attend to. He could squeeze her in and they had lots of fun together talking and laughing. Days later he received a thank you note from her, telling him that she wanted to commit suicide that day but that his joyful energy made her reconsider to keep living instead.

The hairstylist was so right. Not only did he make this woman's day, he saved her life with his joyful nature and care for her. Perhaps that is a good way of picturing the role of a light worker, to make someone's day in whatever function or profession. Spiritual ascendency is a steady upgrade of our vibration. We literally become an ever more potent magnet, emitting positive energies to those who feel drawn in by us. I often refer to our function as light workers, we literally bring the Light into other people's lives.

In the survey of my spiritual friends many reported that they accepted their role in the present ascension wave of sharing the light with others, though some felt a little shy calling themselves light workers. The group of people has many professions and callings in which we have the opportunity to make people's days; such as caretaker of the elderly, restaurant manager, chef, therapist, social worker, author, minister, fisherman, teacher, bus driver, stay at home mom, healer, Reiki- and physical therapist, coach, not-for-profit business owner, medium, coach, psychic, and many others. All of us can be day-makers in our little world of engagement, what is still missing though are the CEOs, the politicians, and other decision makers of our society. Who knows, perhaps that's the next generation of spiritual newcomers. Who knows, perhaps it is you one day.

The hairstylist saved a life by doing his job of cutting hair. That's what light workers can do in the extreme. More generally, they just share positive energy, a few sparks and a little happiness. One friend described his function in the following way in the survey, "*I am not sure I fit the definition of a light worker but I am certainly eager to see people happy and to see them connect to their awareness of spiritual magnificence. I make no overt effort to elicit that happiness, however. I just live filled with happiness and trust that it will spill over to those with whom I have contact."*

I couldn't have stated the role of a light worker any better than that. When I was active in the financial industry my job was to make money for our clients by providing economic and strategy advice. Not a very spiritual calling you might conclude, but then, another responsibility of my job was to build an investment platform of trust and cooperation for a team of 10 experts. That was in fact a spiritual calling and I got many insights as team leader. This was around the time when I wrote my first book, "The Magnificent Experiment". I decided to run a little experiment and entered every strategy discussion with my competitive colleagues under the assumption that they are my friends and that their view was as good as mine, and that the "process" would decide whose view would be chosen. Well, magic happened in these meetings. By disarming myself my colleagues lowered their guards as well and over seven straight years we picked the winning strategy each time. Cooperation beats competition hands down and I felt blessed to have been a living proof of this fact of life.

Our profession should be a place where we can express ourselves creatively. Ideally, it should be something we are talented to do, something we feel passionate about, and a work that gives us purpose and meaning. An added bonus would be if we are also paid well for our services. I picked the story of the hairstylist for a good reason. It was really him who promoted himself to day maker before he realized that he was a life saver as well. You figure out what you are passionate about and what gives you meaning and you go after it. Before you make anyone's day though, make sure that you are making your own day first. I figure the hairstylist felt like an artist at work styling other people's hair, as well as enjoying the social interaction with his clients. Have your eye on your dream job but let life steer you towards it. Often, we don't even know ourselves what makes us truly tick. The awakening journey encourages us to discover who exactly we are at the core of our being. Don't wait for the future though to get there. The job that you are in right now has a spiritual function too. Take my example, working in the financial industry isn't considered very spiritual but it played an important role in my spiritual transformation. Sure, I was a light worker of sorts and made people's days as well, but I also was an analyst who found his authentic voice because of his job.

This is the message of this book, that every moment in your life matters for your spiritual transformation and S-E-L-F expression, whether you perceive it exhilarating, mundane or annoying. Every living moment, professional or otherwise, is an invitation to realize a dimension beyond your self-identification and to be free.

CATCHING THE
ILLUSIONARY SELF

*Enlightenment is not something you achieve. It's
the absence of something. All your life you have
been going forward after something, pursuing some
goal. Enlightenment is dropping all that.*
Charlotte Joko Beck

BREAKING FREE—WE ARE ALL ADDICTED!

The universe is made up of experiences that are designed to burn out your attachment; your clinging, to pleasure, to pain to fear, to all of it. And as long as there is a place where you are vulnerable, the universe will find a way to confront you with it.

Ram Dass

Everyone is addicted! We are simply wired that way. Dopamines are flushing through our brain when we feel pleasure, just as dopamines are withdrawn from our brain when we feel frustrated or disappointed. The ego—our agenda, our cravings, fears and aversions—is hardwired into our body. We are literally addicted to our self! Yet there is a world beyond this compulsion waiting to engage with us, a state where we are in harmony with what is and experience a fulfillment and peace of mind with whatever happens. There is no anticipation of what will be, no hoping for better, and certainly no scheming for a better outcome and no regrets of what was. Life as is generates happiness. This begs the question of course, how exactly do we get there? Unfortunately, sometimes it takes a little pain to start searching for it.

In a recent get together of spiritual friends, I was surprised to learn that nearly half of us had struggled with an addiction or compulsive habits in the past. Others had seen their fair share of pain and trauma as well. I thought this was a curious observation. It is almost as if we are a step ahead of the people who have not yet begun this journey. Something inside of us has broken and we are looking for a new way of putting the pieces back together again. We got an appetizer of what it feels like to be free, and once you have received a taste of peace of mind, you keep searching for that blissful state.

Awakening is a reorientation towards life, a rebirth of sorts. We start emitting different vibrations and our life changes accordingly. A new tribe finds us while some old trusted friends vanish from our life. We are changing job assignments and dump society's expectations of how to live our life. So far so good but I would be careful not to fall into the trap of seeing spirituality as just an invitation to having your own way. The final destination of awakening is the cessation of "me, myself and I" altogether which is an entirely different undertaking than just striving for loving, fulfilled and happy moments all the time. Our mission is to break free from the evolutionary dopamine game for good and every moment counts to get us to that breakthrough stage, even if it is less pleasant than we like. Have a good look at everyone and everything that comes your way no matter whether you feel happy or sad about the situation you are in. If it is happening to you it must be important, otherwise it wouldn't occur. Don't cut off critical voices just because they seem irritating. Don't wish away uncomfortable situations but face them head on and look if something worthwhile comes from them.

Cravings, fears and compulsive actions are wake-up calls. Instead of saying, "Oh, if it wasn't for that longing, I would be free now", ask instead, "What does this compulsive habit have to teach me? Why is my self-identification sticking to it like honey? What am I missing about myself right now?" Addictions and compulsive habits are merely teaching us that the self is still running the show and we can awaken from "me energy" even during these unconscious moments. There is obviously a fine line between the degree of dependency. For the life-threatening addictions, there is only one mission, to beat them and to get your life back. Yet, if the compulsive habit is merely a thorn in your existence then you may have a great opportunity to watch the bio-robot in action. As our degrees of freedom increase, our perceived spiritual struggles can therefore turn into an opportunity instead. Observe the "me energy" in action and get to the source of it. Heal the underlying root cause and step out of the "me energy" altogether.

Dr. Gabor Mate had a curious compulsive habit. Working with drug addicts in Canada, whenever the negative energy of his job got too much for him, he went to the local record store and bought expensive classical CDs. This may seem like a trivial expensive hobby to you, but to him it was a compulsive habit that he wanted to break, especially with his wife complaining about his recklessness. As his credit card bills piled up he decided that he wanted to write his book, "In the Realm of Hungry Ghosts," not only to help his patients who suffered from serious drug addictions but also to show to himself that he could beat his compulsive shopping habit. Well, he sheepishly had to admit at the end of writing his book that he would still purchase way too many classical CDs for his liking.

Dr. Gabor Mate certainly understood what his classical CD fetish was all about. In his messy work environment of addictions and destructive energy he craved a little order, a little beauty. Most likely his compulsive habit just came with his difficult job of being constantly exposed to the dark energies of heroin addiction. Maybe his compulsive habit merely sent him the subconscious message to find a new job. It certainly inspired him to write an important book that helped many others with their addiction and compulsive struggles. I am sure he has long recovered from it, especially because most record stores have closed down anyway and it may not be as much fun to download expensive CD recordings digitally.

What exactly bothers you right now? Maybe you eat or drink too much. Maybe you love too much and go from one romantic relationship to the next. Maybe you enjoy gossiping or watching porn. Maybe you shop compulsively or use social media when you are bored. Maybe you feel small inside so you work hard to be looked up to, or maybe you are so stuck that you feel apathetic about everything and everyone. You know what, so be it! Take the challenge to leave the evolutionary dopamine game behind even if it takes a few years of heavy pushing. Every compulsive habit or addiction can be linked to a trauma that has to be dissolved or a stuck energy—an inner contradiction—that has to be dissolved. There is no alternative but to keep trying to break free. Firstly, your peace of mind and well-being will thank you for it once you have made it safely to the other side. Secondly, you have no choice anyway. In my experience, once the quest towards the Light has started, it cannot be reversed and has to be completed.

All cravings and aversions can be used as a jumping board towards breaking free. In all the striving, transforming and letting go though, please remember the theme of this book. God gave us two eyes, one to watch the compulsive processes at play in order to let go of them, the other to recognize Grace right in front of us. "Me energy"—the craving, the fear, the unconscious repetition—can be spotted in all areas of life, and true freedom is always just one breakthrough away.

LIBERATING AHA-MOMENTS

Make no mistake about it, enlightenment is a destructive process. It has nothing to do with becoming better or being happier. Enlightenment is the crumbling away of untruth. It's seeing through the façade of pretense. It's the complete eradication of everything we imagined to be true.

Adyashanti

God has humor. I was on my way to Philadelphia with a friend for the annual gathering of our spiritual community when I told her about a spiritual aha moment I just had. At that moment, a car passed by with the letters AH (pronounced as aha in German) to confirm its importance. A spiritual aha moment is a breakthrough. We realize that we are leaving a lower plane of consciousness behind and breaking through to a higher level. Our feelings body gets activated during that transformation. Aha transformations are a full body experience. We travel lighter from that day onwards.

I picture spiritual transformation as the layers of an onion. Life peels us like an onion, layer by layer and what we thought we were all about gets removed from us. Extreme changes sometimes leave us naked and vulnerable; like work slumps, illness, or when the love of our life dumps us. As it turns out, spiritual travelers are as vulnerable as anyone when it comes to these life changing ups and downs. There is pain buried in the survey responses that my spiritual friends sent to me. Yet, awakening encourages us to let go. We do not have any regrets as we sooner or later find meaning in the occurrences. We realize that life is designed to expose us to the core of our being so we reach the stage when we start welcoming everything life throws at us with open arms. Some breakthroughs are happy events like the one I experienced with my friend on the car ride to Philadelphia, some less so. Either way, it's the breakthrough that matters, not how we got there. Who knows what exactly triggers an aha moment and the dissolution of something that we had been carrying around? It might be an innocent remark that may be way more meaningful to the receiver than the speaker. It may be a simple occurrence that many don't view as important at all, like the license plate of a car going by. Yet, we are transformed because of it. Take this story as another example of a spiritual aha moment:

A monk decided to try a new meditation spot so he borrowed a boat in a nearby lake and meditated in it in the middle of the lake. He was in deep meditation when he was rudely awoken by a noise—another boat had apparently bumped into him! The monk lost his patience, "Who was stupid enough to disturb his amazing experience?", but when he opened his eyes, he found an empty boat next to his that had apparently drifted out into the lake. This turned out to be a transformative experience for the monk who realized, "There is no other in the boat—the anger is inside of me!"

I have had countless aha moments since my awakening. The citadel called "me energy" is altered with every transformative insight. Perhaps the most transformative insight that revealed my entire misplaced life story up to this point was when I read Suzhen Liu's book, "Letting Go—Release your Suffering" and got stuck on this passage:

We seek recognition by getting better. When do we need to get better? You must have the thought that you were not good enough in the first place if you feel the need to always get better. Whenever we want to improve ourselves, the motivation often originates from the assumption that "I am not good. If I can get better, I won't feel small and I will be seen."

Somehow, I saw my entire life flashing before me at that moment. I realized that with a lot of hard work and chutzpah I had worked myself to the top in graduate school and in my job in the financial industry to get better and more respected every year, and I was just about to do the same in the spiritual community. What a waste of time and energy! It's a mere mind game preventing me from understanding that we are already perfect in the here and now. This was the moment when I broke free from the desire to get better, from the need to be somebody, from the craving to become more widely known in the spiritual community. It freed me from the fear that someone I care about might look down on me and from the quest to be wiser and more enlightened in the future. I was suddenly free from the drive that somehow defined my entire life story. Just like that! It's such a simple insight, and I had likely come across similar statements numerous times, but when I held Suzhen Liu's "Letting Go—Release Your Suffering" book in my hand, my need to be "someone" dropped like a veil.

Understanding that the hunt for recognition is a mental treadmill we can never get off is an insight. It is a sudden shift and we see the world with new eyes afterwards. What I like about these two given examples of self-reflection and transformation is that they both happen while doing other things in life. The monk just wanted to find a new meditation spot and awoke to his anger inside. I wanted to help my spiritual friend get her mentor's book published and awoke to my inner need for approval. That's how spiritual aha moments happen. Life sets us up for them. We receive them just at the moment when they are the most effective learning opportunity. As you read this book, perhaps some words, experiences or stories will light up a transformative aha moment for you as well.

NEVER MIND A
LITTLE MADNESS

> We enjoy lovely music, beautiful paintings, a
> thousand intellectual delicacies, but we have no
> idea of their cost, to those who invented them,
> in sleepless nights, tears, spasmodic laughter,
> rashes, asthmas, epilepsies, and the fear of
> death, which is worse than all the rest.
>
> Marcel Proust

"Am I perhaps going mad?", is a question I sometimes get
when spiritual newcomers ask me for advice. Often my answer
is simply, "No, your monkey mind is just getting the better
of you. A little more sleep, regular meditation and centering
exercises should get you back on your feet. Trust your new-found
powers. They are here for a good reason!" Awakening allows us
to open up to dimensions that few others can experience. It is
only natural that we need a little time to get our arms around
it. It's also a fact that our ego wants to take this new perspective
and run with it. Conspiracy theories abound in the spiritual
community. Some want to embark on a fight of good and evil
that sometimes resembles Star Wars. When I reflect on my
awakening experience with synchronicity I never questioned my
sanity but I was also professionally prepared for sorting through
the random and seeing the essence of the signs that presented
themselves. My job in the financial industry was that of pattern

recognition so my mind had little chance to attack myself over it. Yet, as I previously mentioned, after a few years I did take a conscious step back from looking for them. The Beyond makes Her presence known but once we open up to this new communication channel we do not need to look for anyone or do anything. Everything we ever wanted we already have, always.

We are all born with different abilities and perceptions. Unfortunately, we are still operating in an environment where society doubts the outliers and wants to make them "normal" again. In the awakening survey, there were several women who were born with special spiritual talents but their families frequently put them down over it and even put some in for psychological treatment. Needless to say, it took them a long time to recover from this form of child abuse. The other complicating factor is that for many of us our awakening process coincides with a healing journey. The majority of respondents in the survey said that it was so. Even for me, upbeat as my awakening experience was in 2007-2012, I also suffered from depression and mood swings that were in hindsight caused by my stressful job but were a necessary evil to get a lot of repressed issues and resentment out to the surface. More than once I asked myself whether I could perhaps suffer from bipolar, just as my father did. That's when my spiritual partner showed up who lived on the other side of the planet at the time. She encouraged me to face the inner turmoil and emotional repression and helped me get these fears out in the open. That's the other amazing thing about our awakening journey. When we are ready to break free our support system shows up and guides us through it.

All awakened souls are as sane as they come but it sometimes takes a little struggle to get to that stage. Accumulated karma gets thrown overboard in a series of "dark night of the soul" episodes. These are scary to understand for the rational mind but have to be lived through to align the depth of our subconscious with our conscious understanding. Real physical changes take place in the awakening phase as well. Neural networks get rewired during the kundalini energy expansion and new energy centers open up as healing takes place and the spiritual transformation unfolds. Genius, madness, and spiritual awakening are but a step apart, so we should be patient with ourselves and with others when for a while it looks like we don't have it all together.

One of the sanest and most profound spiritual sages of all times—the 19th century mystic Sri Ramakrishna—spent months in apparent insanity. Yet, the people in his Indian village simply accepted that he was with God at that time. Needless to say, our modern society has no patience for these spiritual time-out periods. So, if you find yourself struggling right now, reach out to the healers and spiritual coaches in your community as well as to the established medical profession. The answer to your struggle will present itself. You are supposed to be awakened from your slumber and pain and encouraged to reposition your life and open up to a new reality that is in plain sight. That's what awakening is all about and yes, you will be as sane as they come.

I remember my "dark night of the soul" moments well. The stress of my work was eating me alive. So many emotions bubbled to the surface. All of my repressed emotions showed up in dreams and sleepless nights. I had panic attacks. I had anger fits. I wanted to numb my mind. Alas, in an awakening journey we can no longer run away. Do you know what I did when I couldn't keep it together during those sleepless nights at 3 am in the morning? I danced! I was literally dancing the night away to Barry White's "Let the Music Play". My family was sleeping at 3 am and no one was watching. Otherwise people certainly would have thought that I had lost my marbles.

A little madness is part of the transformation. So be it. Instead of wishing the irritation away, consider this soul-searching phase as part of the healing. As Marcel Proust observed, in the madness often lies the genius. Or as Tennessee Williams put it, "If I got rid of my demons, I'd lose my angels." Still, don't take the struggle on your own. Reach out to those who can assist you, just as I was blessed to travel my journey with a healer by my side. Sometimes traditional medicine can help to put you in that stage to embark on a healing journey. That proved to be the case for some of the people I worked with without undermining their spiritual awareness. Rest assured that sanity is a signpost of the awakened state. That's what the homecoming journey is all about. We are as sane as it gets, and saner than most.

SPIRITUAL PARTNERSHIPS– FOR BETTER OR WORSE

The new female and the new male are partners on a journey of spiritual growth. They want to make the journey. Their love and trust keep them together. Their intuition guides them. They consult with each other. They are friends. They laugh a lot. They are equals. That is what a spiritual partnership is: a partnership between equals for the purpose of spiritual growth.

Gary Zukav

My first mentee found me years ago. I had exchanged a few messages with her in a spiritual community before and one day she asked me whether I knew anything about twin flames. I had to admit then that I didn't so she told me what she had experienced. She felt a deep emotional connection with someone and experienced everything he was going through, hundreds of miles away. It sounded hard to believe at the time but she convinced me that her experience was true. Her descriptions were just too detailed and precise to be made up. Well, it turned out over the months that even though he had also felt that connection, he in fact had moved on for some reason and started living his own life. She went through hell at that time and I gave her the advice to stay as far away from his energy as possible and to start living her own life. Unfortunately, I couldn't resonate enough with her pain at that time given that I had never experienced such a powerful connection myself.

Years later I met someone else at a spiritual get-together who also admitted that she was in a twin relationship. She said her spiritual partner is married with kids and lived in a town away from her. She said that they rarely communicate but that she can feel everything that he is going through. I replied, "But that sounds awful!" to which she responded dryly, "Yup, a twin flame is a little like sandpaper—it scratches your remaining ego involvement away." The twin flame connection is something some spiritual people encounter. Several of my spiritual friends had a deep spiritual connection with a significant other and had tough choices to face because of it. The heart wants what it wants. When our spiritual significant other shows up we have little choice but to engage and see where the union leads to. Twin flame relationships can be messy, and even poisonous at times; but when they work out, the burning union can catapult both partners to unbelievable heights of Consciousness.

When I reached out to a friend who has written extensively on twin flame relationships and the sacred sexual union between lovers—tantra yoga—to help me with this chapter, she told me that she had moved away from working with people on this confusing subject. "Everyone is just projecting their romantic longings", she said, and true, it's sometimes hard to keep the spiritual dimension apart from the human craving to love and be loved. Yet, the whole purpose of the twin flame connection is to break through to the highest level of Consciousness in the loving union of partners. When it works out we experience bliss and when it doesn't, we discover unconditional love the hard way.

A transformation is always in store because of it. As one survey participant described her twin flame experience, *"The catalyst to awakening was meeting my twin soul in 2011 and having my heart broken wide open into the world of unconditional love."*

I have enjoyed a decade-long partnership with a healer who lived on the other side of the planet when I first met her. She was born in Taiwan and represents Asia, while I was born in Germany and represent the West. We used to be polar opposites in everything. My quest was about finding Oneness in life and finding spiritual messages in all day-to-day occurrences. She found the center of her being in meditation and nature. I have always been a creature of the light while she perks up in rainstorms. In the early years of our interaction we published many notes on wholeness and the Tao Te Ching together. In later years, Suzanne helped me as a healer when my work stress drove me crazy and encouraged me to face my inner pain body. Her biggest contribution in my spiritual growth was to help me understand that I am not my mind. Like the fish that can't experience its water connection without leaving it, I probably never would have realized this on my own.

We both experienced meaningful synchronicities when we met, convincing us that this partnership was worth our attention. The serendipities that we experienced were amazing. I was able to connect with her on my business trips in Asia but the biggest breakthrough in our working relationship happened when serendipity had it that her husband was transferred from Asia to Boston. For a year we were living just a mile apart. Yet, in all the years full of joy, creativity and empowerment, there were also a few frowns and tears. After a while we started going in different directions. At one point, it even looked to me as if we were going our separate ways. "Suzanne stands for sandpaper," I said to her accusingly when we were fighting regularly, to which she replied, "No, Suzanne stands for serenity. Your mind is making up these stories of separation." She was right. We kept our friendship and working relationship intact and recently translated and published the book "Letting Go—Release Your Suffering" together. During the times of struggle Suzanne would often text me out of the blue and ask, "Are you ok?", knowing with an accuracy rate of 100 percent that I was not. When I realized that deep long-distance connection I asked her, "Does that mean that we are twin flames as well?", to which she replied, "I can have this psychic connection with anyone. I only have to tune into the person." Well, that's the power of Oneness that some of us have access to.

There is no question that the union of yin and yang is a powerful magnet and engine that can catapult us into these "out of self" states. I had many personal experiences in that direction and will share an incredible experience in the upcoming chapter about the workings of kundalini energy. Our wholeness begs for the union of the feminine and masculine. That's what the spiritual quest is all about, the transcendence of existing dualities. In a sense, spiritual soul partnerships and twin flame connections are not that different from the traditional guru and disciple relationship, a marriage or the privilege of raising children. It takes a village to lift a soul to ascension. Be glad if you can play your role in helping others and rest assured that love always surrounds you. In all areas of our life, it's a privilege and a blessing to walk that sacred journey with a soul sibling. Take care of your partner and know that you are blessed every moment you travel the journey together.

KUNDALINI AWAKENING
IS A PROCESS

*The spine is the highway to the Infinite. Your own
body is the temple of God. It is within your own
self that God must be realized.*

Paramahansa Yogananda

The other day I was sitting at my favorite Thai restaurant
reading when someone commented on how straight my posture
is. I smiled and replied that I had to. Years ago, when I picked
up golf I had realized how crooked my spine had become so
I did my best to straighten it. She smiled and said that she is
a yoga instructor and has an eye for those things. We have to
watch our posture because that's where the kundalini energy is
flowing. There are yoga disciplines with the aim to stimulate
our energy centers but for me the kundalini expansion has
been a natural process over the years. What I contributed was
rhythmic breathing, walking and sitting straight. This opened
up a spiritual path that continuously encourages me to balance
my chakras. After a twelve-year transformation process I have
received a nice perk that I can consciously activate this energy
with the result that thoughts literally come to a standstill when
this energy reaches my head and serenity prevails for a while.
If you have trouble sleeping, this technique also works magic.
The awakening quest does get easier over the years.

Everything probably started for me in the late 90s when I picked up a book on my travels to India, "Raja Yoga", written by Vivekananda. He advised, besides sitting regularly with an erect spine in a high energy place in meditation, breathing in through the left nostril, and out of the right one. I practiced that over the years and learned to straighten my spine. Then sometime in early 2008 when the before mentioned energy explosion kicked in I was sitting in a conference room with colleagues discussing the end of the world. I felt a bubbling activity in my spine, just at the end of my neck and the beginning of my head area. Energy was flowing through it, which put me in state of serenity and bliss. Around this time my spiritual path opened up as well introducing me to a journey that was simply out of this world.

When spiritual awakening starts, a higher Force puts us on a new trajectory. Kundalini energy is God's plumbing for our energy system so to speak, and She knows what She is doing. The spiritual process is a healing journey and offers a continuous transformation. Energy centers get aligned over the years. Some specialize on aligning energy centers or consciously activating kundalini energy. I often hear questions like "How can I activate my third eye?", "How can I balance my root chakra?", and so forth. I am not sure we need to do anything other than practice mindful living. We literally see Oneness where we struggled with duality before the opening of the third eye. We feel the energy of people and places (opening of the heart chakra), and we know Consciousness (activation of the crown chakra). The energy centers open up in accordance with our spiritual transformation, and spiritual living catapults us to this state.

For me there was a twelve year time span between the time when I got an appetizer of things to come and the year when the kundalini energy broke through in full force. I devoted my entire life to my spiritual journey over this time period whereas the activation of energy centers and neural pathways all happened subconsciously. One of my conscious activities over these years was to become more assertive, and we will come back to this theme in the upcoming chapters on the less pleasant "dark night of the soul" episodes that is unfortunately also part of every awakening. One boon that I have received in my quest, fear has taken a backseat. Awakening has visible perks that will offer gifts for you as well.

Around the time when my heart chakra opened up I also got a taste of how closely the union of yin and yang is connected with the kundalini energy expansion. My friend from the UK with the amazing psychic powers that I mentioned in the introduction of the book texted me one day, "You are ready!" "I am ready," I asked, "ready for what?" She claimed that just based on reading my posts she could sense that my heart chakra was about to open, and she was right. This was at the time when it looked like my spiritual partner and I would be going our separate ways. I lost my sanity for a few weeks. I got a taste of what co-dependency looks like and over those weeks I felt rage, jealousy, and unconditional love all at the same time and in no particular order. This may sound strange but I felt so alive when my heart chakra opened up. My friend from the UK wanted to help me with my heart chakra opening and suggested a phone call. We chatted for an hour, about nothing in particular, just catching up on each other's lives. I remember that day like yesterday. It was in August of 2019. I hung up the phone, got in the car to run an errand and suddenly experienced a massive explosion. The feeling of freedom, serenity and bliss that I had heard about was suddenly there, and different from prior satori moments, it lingered for an entire week. Somehow my friend had activated the kundalini energy, simply by chatting over the phone. That's the power of tantric yoga. Apparently, it doesn't have to be sexual in nature at all.

The biggest perk of kundalini energy awakening is mental serenity. These days my thinking stops for large stretches of time and I often perceive life's events without an agenda, without a thought about what's happening. I am simply watching what's going on as if life is a walking meditation for me. Still, I had my "dark night of the soul" encounters even after that occurrence. Yet, it was a noteworthy breakthrough experience that changed my life for good, and it certainly gave me the authority to share with you the observation that you are already free. Grace is always at our disposal.

These days, whenever the "I" slips back and forth between these different dimensions of experiencing Consciousness, it has become less accidental and random. I am getting triggered less and also don't mind the unconscious moments much. The cloud analogy describes this stage well. We may not always see the sun, but know that these states of being unconscious drift by like clouds in the sky.

You have probably experienced or heard about the kundalini symptoms before—the ringing in the ears, the pressure in the forehead. These aches and pains are all over the place. I also had an unbelievable toothache as the energy got stuck somewhere between the neck and crown area for a few days. Yet, this all sounds worse than it is. For the longest time, I didn't feel anything outside of that bubbly feeling at the top of my spine, and an occasional ringing in my ears. I only panicked one day when a mentee texted me that she felt fluids in her brain and asked whether this was normal. I reached out to a couple of my friends with more kundalini experience at that time and they conjectured that it was possible. My mentee got an MRI done and it returned normal and she has made great strides in her awakening journey in the meantime. There are a few aches and pains associated with building the energy highway of our body and so be it. Once again, God knows what She is doing, but it is reassuring to get a health check-up as well.

Our energy centers open up whenever we are ready to take the next step. The spiritual aha moments come when we are ready for the next transformation and the "dark night of the soul" demons pop up when we are equipped to face them. "Have a little faith that God knows what She is doing," is a comment I repeat often. That's how I have experienced my awakening. We are on track for letting go of our self just like clockwork and every new occurrence faces us exactly at the time when it is meant to. As important as the kundalini energy subject is, it's worth pointing out that in the awakening survey I ran only about half reported meaningful kundalini experiences whereas the rest didn't mention them. Please don't look for something that isn't there. Focus on spiritual living instead.

THE POWER OF SOLITUDE

I find it wholesome to be alone the greater part of the time. To be in company, even with the best, is soon wearisome and dissipating. I love to be alone. I never found the companion that was so companionable as solitude.

Henry David Thoreau

Why do we want to distract ourselves all the time? Why do we want to escape from what we fear we are all about deep inside? Well, it is painful to face ourselves and everything that is hidden there. My awakening started when I was working in a stressful and competitive workplace. I learned that other people were my mirror and they taught me a lot about myself. I loved studying them. I loved all the interactions with everyone. I was riding other people's energies and became quite good at it. I had countless spiritual breakthroughs in these years and shared them proudly in my daily blogs and the first two books. Yet, there was still something missing. As I was facing myself in the outer world, my monkey mind also had plenty of opportunities to keep itself busy by gathering information, contemplating spiritual insights and writing about them. I realized one day that my monkey mind will never go away until I am finally willing to sit down and resist the temptation to do anything and go anywhere. That's what solitude is all about. I realized that I would face stagnation unless I bit the bullet and spent the time with my restless self.

I remember meeting a former colleague who had withdrawn from work earlier than me. We met for lunch and when I was telling her about my plans to become an author and spiritual coach, her response was, "I hope you are prepared for solitude." It seemed such an innocent remark at the time but the moment she said it I knew it would be meaningful for me. Sure enough, experiencing solitude proved much tougher than I expected. All my life it had been more fun for me to fight dragons in the outside world. When I looked inside I discovered so many confusing and frustrating energies such as anger, lack of confidence, ambition, lust, depression, and the desire to be loved and admired. You can fill in the blanks here for whatever it is that is slumbering inside of you. We all have different dragons to slay in the outer world. When we deal with the outer world we can become aware of the drives and fears that rule us. We can express them, transmute them and possibly conquer them. On the outside, we can find a way to make peace with these energies but it is only on the inside that we can truly transcend what is alien to the true center of our being. Yet, this is easier said than done.

Ravi Shankar once said, "Love is seeing God in the person next to you, and meditation is seeing God within us." For me there are two spiritual types, the seekers who still have to face themselves within and the finders who already did. Buddha spent 7 years in the wilderness to find himself. Jesus spent 40 days in the desert. It doesn't matter how long we spend in solitude as long as we have the moment when we look into the abyss and do not budge despite our best judgement. Everything we ever longed for can be found there. The word "al-one" itself implies "all One", or in German—my native language—"ganz allein", all by myself, in contrast to "ganz, allein", whole, all by myself. It's amazing how much spiritual wisdom can be found in each language.

Be still and enter the journey within full of serenity, energy and love. Become restless and observe the void that we normally like to cover upon disguise. It is interesting that even the expression "a void" has the verb "avoid" in it. Facing the void is part of awakening. Try to set yourself free from the bondage of the mind. Otherwise the external world will always take you for a ride. As you are holding this book in your hand, chances are that your mind is just waiting to send you on another quest. After you finish this one, and hopefully find many of the answers that you are looking for, you will get restless once again after a couple of months and will start reading yet another book on how to attain enlightenment, or sign up for yet another lecture. Enough! Put the book away for a couple of days. Go inside. Feel the restlessness. Observe how the mind minds solitude. It is written "be still and know that I Am God" for a reason. When I started my journey inwards I experienced:

L oneliness
E mptiness
B oredom
E nnui

And in the void discovered:

L ove
E piphany
B liss
E nthusiam

These characteristics of "me energy"—loneliness, emptiness, boredom, ennui—are nothing but a façade. They are like bubbles in fact, ready to burst in the intensity of stillness and love. They burst into nothingness when you face the void and love. Epiphany, bliss and enthusiasm appear. The acronym "L-E-B-E" is the imperative "live" in German. In the first stage of our spiritual journey we join life to avoid loneliness, emptiness, boredom and ennui; whereas in the later stage of the awakening journey we are willing to dig deeper and find life itself within us—love, epiphany, bliss and enthusiasm. Under a veneer of the "me energy" there is everything we ever wanted. The Beyond can be found on the inside as well as in real life.

Who is afraid of loneliness if we have solitude to look forward to? May Sarton put this insight beautifully when she writes:

Loneliness is the poverty of self.
Solitude is the richness of SELF.

Enjoy solitude!

TRANSFORMATION

*There is no greater deception than believing that
liberation, which is ever-present as one's own
nature, will be realized at a later stage.*
Ramana Maharshi

ONE HUNDRED PERCENT AUTHENTIC

Our whole spiritual transformation brings us to the point where we realize that in our own being we are enough.

Ram Dass

I remember the brilliance of the sun shining in Boston, Paris and Belgium when my awakening first kicked in. Actually, there was magic in the air pretty much everywhere. There was plenty of laughter and frolicking with my friends. I would never claim for a moment that I am any more awake today as I was then. Yet, something has changed over the years. I am now also able to see the Light within. These days I can consciously activate kundalini energy, whereas then I only felt sporadic surges that left as soon as they came. So, what exactly changes over the years? Not the magnificence of the moment. That will always remain as sparkly as the first day of "Ahhh …" What changes is that we travel lighter. The purging episodes are no longer much of a nuisance and one day we finally understand what they are all about. We keep letting go of this illusionary self as it pops up. Removing the conditioning that we carry around, layer by layer, until we penetrate to the core of our being almost naturally. We get more bold, more humble and humorous. It also gets much easier to forgive, ourselves as well as others.

There is a big inconsistency between the perennial truths that our sages communicate and the awakening experience many of us have. We experience awakening as a process, a quest, a healing and growth opportunity; whereas the message of the sages is that we are only fooled by our mind. "What journey and what transformation?", they say, "You are climbing an imaginary mountain". It's true what they say, I experienced it myself. So, in all the climbing don't forget to stop now and then and smell the flowers. You have arrived already! Please don't miss out on the ever-present Light in your life because you are too busy healing, growing and sharing the gospel with others. Focus on being authentic—just be—and let the Beyond do the rest.

Pema Chodron writes:

Welcome the present moment as if you had invited it. It is all we ever have so we might as well work with it rather than struggling against it. We might as well make it our friend and teacher rather than our enemy.

A life motto of spiritual travelers!

Authenticity is one of these expressions we all love to use but no one really knows what it means. Maybe "Buddhist therapist" Mark Epstein comes closest to getting his arms around it in his essay "Already Free" when he says that there is a part of our being that never changes over time. I remember meeting my two roommates from graduate school over beer after I had already been working in the financial sector for a few years. One of them turned to me with a big smile, exclaiming, "You haven't changed at all!" I knew what he meant then. It was that light-heartedness, a certain good-naturedness, perhaps even naivety on my part. Well, as it turned out, I did lose it in the ensuing years when the stress of my work got to me but then made a comeback with a vengeance when my awakening kicked in. So, what if we lose our authenticity now and then? At least we got a good look at our illusionary self and will afterwards make darn sure that it never happens again. When I reflect on my spiritual friends these days, many of them feel quite happy in their skin. They are authentic and build their life around who they are rather than the other way around.

Authentic living is the ability to be part of Oneness without any self-imposed interferences. Life merely flows through us like Light is reflected in a prism. We still imprint our idiosyncratic color but it is the Light that shines. We are merely the vessel. Life responds to our vibrations and aligns with what we are all about. Work, friends, our significant other; everyone allows us to be. The difference between a novice and a seasoned traveler is the ability to return to the center of our being more quickly as we once again realize our unconscious reaction patterns. What was days or weeks of purging around the dawn of our awakening becomes minutes or hours for the more seasoned traveler. We are also not any more holy or smarter than the fellow next door but we have a more experienced eye for the spirit messengers. We know that tingle in our crown chakra when Spirit is talking, or recognize the desperate voice in our head or the knot in our stomach that tells us our narrow self has taken over the steering wheel once again. Externally, we have the ability to see agendas at play that often include our own. We suddenly see Spirit messengers where we saw friends and enemies before. Internally, we no longer mind when our little self cries murder and opens up to healing and forgiveness instead. Rain or shine, we have a shot at being aware. There comes a stage for many of us when we just enjoy the ride no matter what life throws at us. We are one hundred percent authentic.

LET GOD MAKE YOU SPECIAL

Cause I gonna make you see,
there nobody else here,
no one like me.
I'm special, so special.
I gotta have some of your attention,
give it to me!

Brass in a Pocket, Pretenders

It's such a joy to be smarter than the fellow next door, or to be the high school homecoming queen, or to have that mansion that everyone else can only dream about. You fill in the dots please and tell me what gets your juices going, or once did. The craving of the self—just as the fear of not getting what we are all about—has a taste, has a smell, has a rush of testosterones and dopamines associated with it. You know when you are "on", just as you unmistakably know when something is missing.

I remember the joy that went through me when someone in the spiritual community posted a note claiming that the old villain "ego" was in fact our life force, and that trying to kill it was equivalent to suicide. Though an unpopular idea in our community, I just knew that it was right. Each of us has access to a stream—a life force—that needs creative expression. The problem only before was that we disagreed with life, in which direction it should be headed. Our illusionary self wanted to impose a personal will on life. The answer is to drop everything that is superimposed on us, as life takes us places and we manifest what we are all about. Jump into the stream that nourishes the garden you are creating.

Specialness separates us while our uniqueness unites us with others and the higher dimension that is always at our disposal. The learning opportunity is knowing which is which. If we feel great about ourselves we might again have stepped on someone else's toes; but then, if we feel depressed, we may not express what we are all about. Self-discovery can be a balancing act at times. Still, I always recommend to everyone who asks, express your uniqueness in all areas of your life and let purpose find you. Finding our uniqueness is a two-way process. We have to be open to life's feedback mechanism as well as discover what's meaningful to us. Being the lead violin is great if it is embedded in an orchestra with a talented conductor. Spiritual living is following our life's energy and creatively expressing it.

Awakening, with all the joys and magic it brings, also feels a little like purgatory. It's like an engine dying within us. We still feel the old desires of being special but we can't express them any longer. On the other hand, we already taste and see the garden that is out there for each of us but we are still not quite there either. We are in no man's land, damned if we do and damned if we don't. This part is just a phase, a re-orientation of sorts. We get there sooner or later. The quicker you are able to let go of all self-imposed resistance, the sooner it will come.

The Course in Miracles promises about the state to come, *"And you will think, in glad astonishment, that for all this you gave up nothing.*" It's like someone pulled a lever, replacing co-dependent love with universal love, passion with enthusiasm, and fear of losing out with the knowledge of always having. The ego's trusted allies and villains fall like dominos and are replaced with the four pillars of S-E-L-F: Serenity, Energy, Love, and Flow.

You know when the shift into the new world is complete but until then just keep planting your garden. Let God make you special.

EMPOWERMENT AND SELF-EXPRESSION

The oldest and strongest emotion of mankind is fear, and the oldest and strongest kind of fear is the fear of the unknown.

H. P. Lovecraft

She was a good woman. She raised two girls who inspired by her tenacity and appreciation for knowledge made it all the way to the Ph.D. level half way across the world. She herself got bitter though as the decades went by and the girls left the house. She blamed her conservative family for not allowing her to go to Radcliffe to study. She blamed her husband for not supporting her enough when she could have been a psychology counselor at a school. Yes, her loved ones could have been more supportive but she also could have claimed that chutzpah that she instilled in her daughters. Had she only stood up to her fears, and her misplaced emphasis on loyalty, her own experience of suffering and scarcity might have been the realization that abundance always surrounded her.

The dilemma of this loyal woman was a lack of self-empowerment and a missed opportunity for self-expression. Many of us struggle with that problem. I am certainly no exception. The biggest enemy was always fear—fear of not being empowered and fear of not being admired. Yet life was kind to me. Over the years I managed to surround myself with people who are not shy to kick me in the behind when I am not living up to the challenge of the moment. She didn't dare to stand up to the people closest to her as she felt a well-behaved Indian wife, mother and daughter wouldn't do that. It may have been misunderstood loyalty and she may not have been loyal enough to the person who mattered the most—herself.

It's a joy to see people who leave their little self behind and feel universally empowered. They have conquered their fears. When they see littleness and limited mindsets, they turn away in disgust. They don't take anything away from others because they are too busy creating something way more powerful. Many of my friends and loved ones have made the jump from little self to universal empowerment. In fact, anyone who signs up for a spiritual journey is bound to get there. Sometimes we merge with the Beyond because we can feel its energy, and sometimes we stand up to our fears and limited "me energy" because that's what an inner voice encourages us to do.

A spiritual life empowers us to dump the dictate of our limited beliefs. Empowerment and self-expression come easily to us because we serve naturally, and in turn experience abundance and freedom. We vibrate higher as we serve others who in turn raise us. The little stream becomes a rampant river that finally merges with the ocean.

In my experience life coaching is as important as spiritual coaching. Life encourages us naturally to express ourselves authentically but there are always areas where littleness rules us. Sometimes spirituality itself, or rather our understanding of it, is the problem statement. "Sex is not spiritual", some religious voices say, even though it is the physical expression of love and the biggest creative force there is—the creation of a new life. "You are supposed to love your neighbor as yourself," the Bible says, even though quite frankly, we can't stand him. The unwillingness of the obedient daughter to stand up to her conservative mother when Radcliffe invited her to come to Cambridge, Massachusetts was one such example. Coaches help folks claim their natural power as we encourage them to find their authenticity and passions. We know what we are talking about because many of us had to take the same scary jump into the unknown and live to tell others about it.

	self	Consciousness	
	"Poor	Light	
suffering	me"	worker	service
	"Came, saw,	Follow	
abuse	conquered"	the Signs	abundance

The difference between self and Consciousness can always be felt by the energy someone emits. It was only after my awakening when I understood that there is no difference between aggressiveness—the abuse of others—and passive aggressiveness—the abuse of our self. Littleness is behind the attack, as well as cowardice. The feeling of empowerment is quite different. When we use universal power, there is no difference between serving others and receiving abundance. In a world of Oneness, giver and receiver are the same.

Are you ready to connect with your universal power base? Do you still have areas of scarcity and littleness in your life? Are you ready to sign up for the magnificence of empowerment and self-expression?

BREAKING FREE FROM INNER CONFLICTS

The greatest courage is not in fighting outside battles but in addressing the source of conflict within yourself.

Sadhguru

You probably know the feeling of having needles under your skin. You are unsure whether to turn left or right, fully knowing that no matter what you do, you will likely not be satisfied with either scenario. What is it that troubles you? You can't live with or without your significant other? You don't know whether to go for that promotion or enjoy your peace of mind? You wonder whether now is the time to go after your dreams but you don't know where the money will come from? Our spiritual community tends to give black and white answers such as, "You have to follow your heart", or "You have outgrown your unconscious partner", "Stand up to your fears and follow your dreams." This advice may be right or it may not be. I recommend taking a step back first and appreciate the conflict as is—hard as this is to accept. Maybe there is a chance to find your authentic self by squaring the circle. Maybe you are encouraged to express yourself authentically by facing the catch 22. Maybe you realize that there is a giant hole in the story you like to tell yourself and manage to stop story telling period. Maybe the tension of holding on to two opposing forces breaks something open inside that allows you to connect to a higher dimension of being. So maybe there is no solution to your inner conflict at all, but in the moment of dismay you finally meet your "me energy" in action and manage to have an epiphany realizing Oneness is hiding within the mistakenly-perceived conflict. In Oneness, all conflict is naturally dissolved.

Why complain about mission impossible? Isn't dropping the story we tell ourselves in our head what our spiritual mission is all about? Discover why your personal conflict was hand delivered to you, inviting you to be free. What inner tensions do you have right now? I used to have many inner conflicts and perhaps worst of all, I wasn't even willing to admit them to myself. Awakening confronts us with all inner conflicts and brings them out in the open. These problems and conflicts are there to encourage us to do more than just solve them. The goal of awakening's transformation is that we are open to life as a free and authentic person, erasing all self-imposed limitations. It's not that hard to see that life constantly confronts us with the homework we still have to tackle to remind ourselves of all remaining inconsistencies. It is us sending little messages to ourselves, "Hey, look here, how can you have peace of mind unless you tackle this problem statement?" My spiritual breakthrough happened when I realized that every "problem" is a present in disguise.

Life becomes a lot more fun when you approach it with a curious mind. Suddenly, messengers that were avoided before become allies because we know that they bring us another missing piece of the puzzle. I was born with a hunger for recognition without really admitting it to myself. At school,

I always had to be the best and figured it was my noble thirst for knowledge. At work in the competitive financial industry I was egged on to be the best at what I did and I took up the challenge with feverish excitement. It was only 10 years into my job that I noticed a curiosity in myself. I realized that I had literally two separate prevailing inner natures—the competitive and collaborative energies that got activated by different people and problem statements. The nature of my work made me acknowledge the competitor in me, even though it wasn't a very spiritual thing to do. That's perhaps why I had repressed it most of my life. Since that realization I have become a big believer in embracing what life brings my way, not what I want to see or aspire to have. Life is designed to help us discover who we truly are and should be respected as such even if we do not like what we see. So, if you find yourself in a difficult situation, ask yourself how this problem statement can help you finding your authentic self, rather than wishing it away.

Once the dirty secret was out in the open—I am competitive— everything became much easier for me. I had a spiritual breakthrough and used the different energies quite effectively. I wore the competitive hat of an analyst when it came to giving specific strategy recommendations to our portfolio managers. But then, spending a couple of decades with the same experts covering the world economies, I also had the chance to develop my collaborative nature. I lead the group of experts in a setting of trust, appreciation and cooperation and regularly wrote up our joint insights which was a precursor for my writing career. My boss half-jokingly called me a Zen investor with a German accent. He was right, literally and figuratively.

The strangest thing was that as I finally had the guts to admit the competitive nature to myself, I realized that success meant much less to me than I would have thought. Whenever I was finally in the limelight, it was a good experience but not so great that it was worth running after. After needing years to even admit the hunger for power, name and fame for myself, I spent as many years getting there but then feeling empty upon receiving it. Then the solution to my inner struggle presented itself. I realized that what made me truly happy was developing one meaningful connection at a time: one client, one investor, and one friend at a time proved to be my recipe for success. I don't know if you have observed this but in the magnificence of the here and now, the "me, myself and I" energy tends to melt in an ocean of Oneness. Being with people, or doing what I am passionate about, always has this impact on me.

Today I have switched professions and callings, but I kept my recipe for success and happiness. I am still surrounded by good friends today just as I was in my profession before. Even today it is one client, one reader and one spiritual friend at a time. Today I write books. I help clients with their spiritual mission and I build a community with my friends to promote spirituality, wholeness and healing. "What conflict of interest?" I ask myself today. Life is good!

The Course in Miracles reminds us:

We must open all doors and let the Light come streaming through. There are no hidden chambers in God's temple.

This is a really important observation. We cannot be half free or 90 percent free. Clouds come and go, but the authentic self has to be free of conflicts and pure; a powerful conductor of the higher energies. We have to be absolutely free of all self-induced interferences and there is only one way to get there, to let life tell us what is still missing. What is a "dark night of the soul" episode but tantrums the self is throwing to tell us that the story we tell ourselves still has holes in it. Had I set out to become a monk before my combative friends in the financial industry had a chance to hold up a mirror for myself, I would have been miserable. My life would have been a waste! That's what all of life's challenges are about, to show us the areas where we still have a little work to do. Discover yourself, express yourself and then lose your self in the magnificence of the now or the silence of your being.

Everything life throws at us is a learning opportunity. Everything, and we might say, "everyOne", holds up a mirror for us and invites us to be free. What conflict? It's just another opportunity to be free.

TRANSFORMATION IS FOUND IN THE EYE OF THE STORM

Enlightenment, the meaning of that word is, a mind that has no conflict, no sense of striving, going, moving, achieving.

J. Krishnamurti

Most people have probably experienced a taste of "cessation of self" after an earth shattering orgasm. We see a light flashing and our thoughts stand still. There is a feeling of fulfillment, serenity and love as we melt in the arms of our exhausted lover, but then, when we open our eyes again, the old world is back just as we left it. It is the same with the satori moment, we are so captured by nature or the beauty of a moment that we get awed into silence. A day or two later, unfortunately, that experience is also a distant memory.

Witnessing Awareness is a serene feeling without experiencing any thoughts. It's the moment in time when the right half of our brain is in accord with the left side and is still. It's the blessed state when the mind finally hugs the heart. We are back to the part of the wholeness we once came from. It's a full body experience that is an "out of self" experience at the same time. From a mind perspective, the word epiphany is the best approximation of that blessed stage. For a moment, the mind understands the game it had been playing all along and quiets down in awe and respect. From a feelings perspective, the repressed pain body erupts like a volcano and vanishes. Finally, there is peace.

Life gets us to this blessed state. It confronts us with the inner conflicts we have to tackle. It invites us to understand the workings of our mind, the conditioning that we have accepted as ourselves. Awakening can feel like an obstacle course that prepares us for these breakthroughs. These moments of truth can be best compared to the eye of the storm. I got this graphic below from my friend Melissa Pope who also participated in the survey. It explains how amidst life's many agitations, we often have the most amazing breakthrough experiences. The inner conflicts get resolved in one big eruption. A light bulb goes off and we see that our aggression is really the fear of losing out. Our pride and drive is the fear of being powerless. Our laziness and negativity is really the fear of getting started. It takes the turbulence of life to bring our pain body and our self-imposed limitations to the surface. We face the pain, we digest it, and feel miserable doing so but the next morning brings the blue sky. Once the storm is over we have lost yet another piece of our illusionary self.

Awakening Spiral

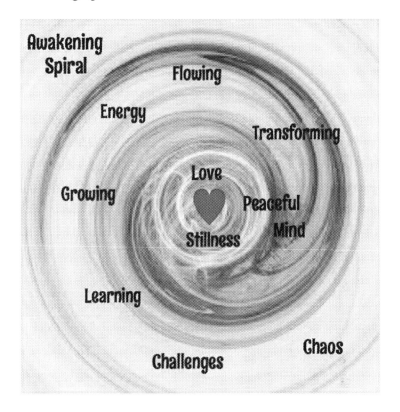

The problem with the enlightenment concept is that it generates the impression that after reaching this state there is peace, love and bliss until the end of time. It may therefore become a projection, a never ceasing dangling of the carrot in front of the donkey's nose, never to be reached. Instead we should view the eye of the storm just like we enjoy a mind blowing orgasm. It shouldn't prevent us from having another one. The Beyond will always be, well, beyond us. We have the challenge and the creativity of the here and now to look forward to for the rest of our life. There is an ongoing invite to dance with life. The here and now is always as good as it gets. In Adyashanti's words:

It is true that, after awakening, the exterior situations and circumstances of life stop having such an ability to throw us off center. But it's also true that, when we awaken, we start to become more conscious of the patterns of behavior in our lives that are not in harmony with what we have realized. If you believe the misperception that enlightenment is only about happiness, bliss, and freedom, you will be motivated to transcend or escape those areas of your life that feel less than fully functional. Sooner or later, as we become more awake, we find that there is more and more pressure to encounter and deal with those areas of our lives that we have been avoiding, where we are less than fully conscious.

The truth of the matter is that once the awakening process kicks in we are still invited to be Home in every moment. We just have a little homework to do when the rain clouds set in and we have to sow seeds into the ground for the next harvest. So never mind the emotional hurricane season, transformation is found in the eye of the storm. Jump right in!

THE DARK NIGHT OF THE SOUL: PURGE, ALIGN, RINSE AND REPEAT

I met a woman in the Spiritual Awakening Group a few years ago who wanted to know what the "dark night of the soul" was all about. I told her that if she feels called to face the Light, she is also bound to face resistance in the so perceived dark corner of her being. As it turned out, a lot of stuff came to the surface in her particular case such as abuse, trauma, addiction, and the economic and emotional struggle of being a single parent. The pain she had to face was immense. Often, she reached out to me with the regularity of the full moon cycle, asking how to stop the pain.

Everyone who is on a conscious journey towards the Light has to deal with the problem that the pain body of the past—our hurts of the past and not so kosher cravings and inner conflicts are bound to rise to the surface. The key is to sign up for a healing journey, to confront the inner conflicts as best as we can but also to use this opportunity to accept who we truly are and to forgive ourselves and others as best as we can. Accepting the "dark night of the soul" as the price to pay for the awakening is only one step towards healing and wholeness. There are many more. Our authenticity lies in this dark corner of our soul. The quicker we are willing to shine the light towards it and open up for healing, the faster and more potent our transformation will be. Especially for some spiritual folks who often miss out on being authentic because they want to live up to some lofty spiritual ideals. Even more than that, it is especially in these rebellious phases when we can see the "me energy" at work. Watch it without condemnation. Forgive and love the parts of you that you previously disowned and you might be granted another priceless "out of self" moment. This happened to me so I know that it is true.

A friend came up with this neat description of the "dark night of the soul" ascension transformation:

> *Purge*
> *Shift*
> *Align*
> *Rinse*
> *Repeat*

Make purging part of the process. We all have our idiosyncratic troubles: lost love, career challenges, economic problems, missed creative expressions, abuse, trauma or addictions. Sometimes we can find a solution for what troubles us. Sometimes we have to figure out how to let go of the pain. There are superb healers in our community who can help you let go of a painful past. There are also life coaches who can help you face your personal challenges. I see my contribution as a spiritual coach in helping you understand that the "dark night of the soul" is a distorted vision of an immensely creative process. Chances are that there is a part of you that isn't authentic yet. Until the day when you manage to own up to it, these monsters from the depth of your being are bound to return.

Continents are shifting constantly, and earthquakes and volcanic eruptions are necessary stress relievers to keep the movement going. The "dark night of the soul" is an opportunity to let go and to become more authentic in the journey towards the Light. There is opportunity in every crisis. These days when I see pictures of the friend who used to reach out to me to ask for help a few years ago, I see acceptance and a new found beauty. Something for sure shifted within her.

SHADOW WORK: MIND THE GAP!

One of my first Buddhist teachers, Jack Kornfield, writes very movingly in his book "A Path with Heart" about his early experiences in long term meditation at a monastery in Thailand. His mind was just filled with lust. He was freaking out about it, but his teacher just told him to note it. Despairing that it would never change, he tried his best to follow his teacher's instructions. And what he found was that, after a long period of time, his lust turned to loneliness. And it was a familiar loneliness, one that he recognized from childhood and that spoke of his feeling of not being good enough, not deserving enough of his parent's love. I think he said something like, "There's something wrong with me, and I will never be loved." Something like that. But his teacher told him to stay with those feelings, too; just to note them. The point wasn't to recover the childhood pain, it was to go through it. And eventually the loneliness turned into empty space. While it didn't go away permanently, Jack's insight into something beyond the unmet needs of childhood was crucial. This is one way to unhook ourselves from repetitive, destructive, addictive desire. It lets us go in a new direction—it frees desire up.

Mark Epstein

Everyone who embarks on a spiritual quest has a dark corner of the soul where the demons are howling: addiction, abuse, lost love, co-dependency, lust, work, laziness, craving for name and fame; the list of possibilities is endless. Shadow work is the ability to zoom into the trouble spot and dissolve the gordian knot of entangled cravings and painful memories of the past. There are really two dimensions to getting the job done. First, be mindful of the jumps in thoughts and feelings when the problem area gets activated. Mind the gap, so to speak. The experience of Jack Kornfield is a great example in this direction. One day allowing the sex demons to roam freely, he realized that his never ending lust was in fact related to a childhood memory of not experiencing his parent's love. Observe when these jumps take place. Say for example you are thinking of work one moment and of sex the next, what is the missing theme in that mental jump? For me these associations have often been about power, but that's just me. We certainly all have our own self-centered connections. Just observe your mind and feelings as you make these jumps.

The second dimension of the problem statement is how can we in fact dissolve these entangled cravings and memories so that the "desire energy" can move freely again, just as it does in all other areas of our life. Therapy can help with that, as can mindfulness. Observe how you feel, what triggers you, what memories pop to the surface, and so forth.

A powerful letting go method is presented by Qigong Master Suzhen Liu in "Letting Go—Release Your Suffering", which is the book I had the pleasure to introduce to the Western world. In it, Suzhen Liu offers specific exercises that allow you to discover what repressed feelings and pain bodies are buried in the depth of your being and shows concrete examples of how to release them. Our spiritual community unanimously declares our mind to be the villain standing in the way to enlightenment and they are certainly right on one level. Yet, no one is able to show you how to make it to the stage of having a still mind since they are missing out on the feelings dimensions and how to address stuck energies and pain bodies of the past. Suzhen Liu's work can help get you to this level. She herself reached enlightenment after a number of deaths took place in her family over a very short period of time while she herself was facing cancer. She broke down and cried for an entire week and somehow managed to break free from that prior self-identification in the free-flowing tears. This mirrors my experience too. Amazing spiritual breakthroughs can occur when we truly open up to what slumbers in the depth of our being without resisting it.

FINDING GEMS IN
THE SHADOW

*Out beyond ideas of right doing and wrong doing
there is a field.* I'll meet you there.

Rumi

I have had my fair share of "dark night of the soul" struggles,
and based on the survey results it is safe to say that almost
everyone faces a soul-searching transformation during an
awakening. Sure, it is uncomfortable when the repressed stuff
from the past and the misunderstood ambitions bubble to the
surface but there is also incredible creativity bubbling in the
depth of our being. The sooner we open up to it, the faster and
more powerful the transformation will be.

At the onset of my spiritual awakening I had a strange dream. I
was in a vacation resort when I heard on the radio that convicts
had broken out from a nearby prison. I looked around and saw
a group of them approaching me. "Look", someone shouted,
"There is fresh meat." I ran away and someone followed me.
I ran into a building and somewhere on the second floor he
caught up with me. We wrestled and both crashed through
a window onto a balcony. That was the first time I had a
good look at him. He was as tall as me, with body builder
muscles and a clean shaven head. His face looked grotesque as
he wrestled me. He looked just like I would imagine a demon

to look like. Amazingly, despite his intimidating look, I could keep him at arm's length fairly easily. The calmer I got, the more furious he became. Then I woke up. I felt peaceful, even happy, not knowing why.

It took me a while to understand what this dream was all about. A few months later childhood memories started popping to the surface and I understood what my upcoming transformation was all about. The demon in the dream just mirrored back to me my suppressed aggressiveness. I realized that I was effectively a lion raised by lambs. Not aggressive enough to stand up for what was meaningful to me I had to resort back to passive aggressiveness. Yet, the job I was in was perfectly designed to help me step it up a bit. Every year my voice became a little louder and every year I leaned a little more out of the window to make my ideas heard. As the years went by, the demon and I made up. I even have a name for him, my inner *Kerl*, German, for fellow.

Many folks in our community are a bit conflicted just like I used to be. It is the pain of running constantly into a wall that makes us wake up one day searching for a new way. Amazingly, that's exactly the time when glimpses from the depth of our subconscious being start to appear. Unfortunately, it can be a bit confusing to embark on a spiritual journey with one foot still in the old world and one in the new world. There are plenty of self-imposed interferences. Our super ego tells us what it means to be spiritual. We judge others and ourselves. We administer "Thou shall do that" and "Thou shan't do that" rules and may even succeed in living by them but we end up living like zombies.

God doesn't judge. Why should we? For me personally, I realized in that transformation process that situation specific assertiveness is not in conflict with spirituality at all. As a matter of fact, there are times when life encourages me to put my foot down and I mostly do it now with a lot of gusto. Lion and lamb can lie together peacefully, just as it is written in the Bible. I never saw the demon again but I have made a career for myself thanks to his insistence to bring my competitive nature and hidden aggressiveness out there and let it work for me. In that way, I learned not to be afraid of the dark side but rather view it as an opportunity to be my authentic self.

There are libraries written about the shadow process and how to cope with the "dark night of the soul" episodes. If you want to learn more about it, I recommend reading Debbie Ford's, "The Dark Side of the Light Chaser." It was amazing that it took one simple dream interpretation for me to steer my life into a completely new direction, even though, as mentioned, the process of resolving my inner conflicts took many years. Spiritual travelers have creative tools at their disposal. My favorite story was that of the Swiss author Kim-Anne Jannes who claimed that her demon transformed into a beautiful dragon that protected her from evil of all sorts. How amazing is that! I would echo her conclusion. When you have the guts to look in the dark corner of your soul, a gem is waiting for you.

GLIMPSES OF S-E-L-F

Get lost in a mission.
Melt in the arms of your beloved.
Dissolve in the magnificent moment.
Be still, and know "I Am That I Am!"
Transcending our illusionary self
Is Home—so get lost!
Christian M. Wiese, "Get lost and be found".

THE PASSION TEST

Ignoring your passion is slow suicide.
Never ignore what your heart beats for.

Unknown

It was a summer when the boys were still quite young and my sister-in-law was staying with us to help the two working parents out. At the end of her stay there was a foul mood in the house. We were all tired of each other. I remember a car ride we took together to Boston when somehow, we got in an argument. I can't even remember what started it or what it was about but somehow there was an explosion in the car, a thundering lightning bolt so to speak. My sister-in-law and I were both screaming. I was banging the steering wheel in frustration and my wife who hates conflict was looking helplessly at the two of us fighting. It was the first time that I ever experienced a thunderbolt like that. As it turned out, I was discharging stale energy. The fight wasn't about my sister-in-law at all and truly, I can't even remember what the fight was about. After a few minutes of screaming and banging the steering wheel it was simply gone and the sun started shining again. What I do remember about the argument, however, was that my sister-in-law accused me of being out of touch with my passions and she was absolutely right.

My spiritual journey had started in earnest but at work I was not as effective as I could have been. I was doodling around, following my own research agenda which was out of touch with what my constituents wanted from me. The irony was that this fight was just around when my life took off in all directions so my sister-in-law just caught me when old stale energy wanted to exit my system. In the spiritual realm, I met my spiritual partner who jump started my transformation by showing me that I am not my mind. Professionally, everything started to come together. All of a sudden my line of research became cool and I spent as much time developing my own voice as an investor as building a research platform of collaboration and team work within the group I was working for.

A spiritual transformation is just like the metamorphosis of a caterpillar into a butterfly. There is a period of rest, listlessness and apparent stagnation. I often hear people complaining about how they struggle professionally and economically because of this lack of focus and direction. I offer this recommendation: reconnect with your passions but also don't forget about your talents. The spiritual purpose and professional calling will find you, and you don't have to worry about money either. In my case, the timing of my breakthrough was very interesting. While my spiritual maturity started taking off and I was even given a great opportunity to express it professionally in a very competitive work place by building a platform of mutual trust and cooperation, it was also the time when I could express my own competitive juices as an investor which few would consider very spiritual. Yet, that's where my passions were hiding as well.

We get this question often, "I don't feel satisfied with my work and I don't have much money either. Should I quit everything and follow my passions?" Well, I don't know but I am reminded of what my astrologer said when I posed the same question. I asked whether it was time for me to embrace my calling as an author, educator and spiritual coach. She said, "You know when the time is ripe. You just know it." She was right. A couple of years later I quit my profession of 22 years and launched my spiritual endeavor instead. There are really four considerations at work: do what you love doing, do what you are good at, do what you can be paid for and do what the world needs. We had two young kids when my awakening started. I had bills to pay, and that's why I stayed at my job and it was the best thing that ever happened to me. Yet, recently I had a long conversation with a spiritual friend who did exactly the opposite. With two little kids to look out for he decided to leave his established profession and become a life coach full time. Good for him. There is obviously no right or wrong. There is only the path that works for you. Earning a livelihood is important but always keep an eye out for what makes you come alive.

> *Don't ask what the world needs. Ask what makes*
> *you come alive, and go for it. Because what the*
> *world needs is people who have come alive.*
> Howard Thurman

At the firm, I used to work for, my colleagues never talked much about what would be next in store for them after retirement. Maybe it was because they already had put their hearts and souls into their life work so that it was hard for them to imagine what else there could be, or maybe it was because some of them had become so rich that they were looking forward to finally spending it. Whatever the reason was, the standard response at the farewell party was, "First I take six months off and then we'll see." One colleague was different though. He only smiled knowingly when I asked him what would be next for him but he didn't tell me either. Apparently, he was too embarrassed. Later over dinner, however, he mustered his boldness and revealed to everyone that he would become a painter. The room was stunned.

The wife of a friend is an art curator. She had a look at his first painting and later said in private, "This painting is so bad, it is almost good!" Well, the newly minted painter couldn't be discouraged by the naysayers. He took classes, learned some new techniques, and experimented with them. He kept going no matter what the critics said. Years later I met someone who had seen his more recent paintings and remarked that they were quite good. The art curator also had a look at his paintings in later years. She mused that in fact there was something refreshing about his first painting that the acquired technique in later years took a little away from the original boldness. Still, she also admitted that his paintings had gotten much better over time. So, like my impressive colleague beforehand, if you feel that you have something important to share, do it!

We function just like an iceberg. We think we know what we want but this is only 10 percent of our being. Deep down there is stuff waiting to come to the surface that we know little about. Amazingly, it is 90 percent of our being and we have to be humble enough to listen to its message, as well as skilled enough to let it rise out of the depth of our being. Don't worry.

Life will be happy enough to introduce your true being to you. Follow your passion. Focus on what makes you tick but don't neglect what you are good at either. You were given these talents for the reason to express yourself creatively and passionately. I thank my sister-in-law to this day for giving me the kick in my backside when I had reached a low point in my career and life journey. It jump-started an amazing ride.

FEEL THE FEAR, TASTE THE CRAVING AND GO BEYOND

Is fear really a bad thing?
Something "I" need to get rid of?
I hold my fear in my arms,
Gaze into her eyes,
Understand her vulnerability,
And then I go beyond!

I am neither this,
nor that,
I Am That I Am!

Suzanne Yang

When my heart chakra opened up with a bang, I could feel the after effects of a kundalini breakthrough linger for an entire week. Blissfully I walked around mumbling to myself, "The spiritual revolution is here and now!" That state is long gone now. How to get it back? Yet, is there even a need to get it back? We can be aware in the here and now, even if the self still has a few layers of illusion to shed. Yes, there is the satori moment that takes our breath away, the feeling of love and Oneness that we are often blessed with. Yet, the bliss and love experienced in the outer world is only part of life—Awareness is also present as the self struggles with anxiety, fear, greed, lust, or whatever else may be bothering you. We can always be present with life; independent of whether we like the state that we are in or not.

The moment when the fears or the longings of the "I" want to take us for a ride is the perfect opportunity to reconnect with "I Am That I Am" once again. The 13th century poet and mystic Rumi puts the "I Am That I Am" experience beautifully in "The Guest House":

> This being human is a guest house.
> Every morning a new arrival.
> A joy, a depression, a meanness,
> some momentary awareness comes
> as an unexpected visitor.
> Welcome and entertain them all!
> Even if they are a crowd of sorrows,
> who violently sweep your house
> empty of its furniture,
> still, treat each guest honorably.
> He may be clearing you out
> for some new delight.
> The dark thought, the shame, the malice,
> meet them at the door laughing and invite
> them in.
> Be grateful for whatever comes,
> because each has been sent
> as a Guide from beyond.

I always took Rumi's Guest House as an invite for mindfulness and judgement-free living. Yet, it is so much more. Rumi is effectively telling us how to experience Awareness. A fear is creeping up inside, we feel the "me energy" in motion and by realizing it, the energy vanishes as quickly as it came. We look in the mirror and see a self-aggrandizing posture or a deflated look and once again, we see the "me, myself and I" energy in action. One giant smile and we connect with the center of our being once again.

Feel the fear, taste the craving, find the center of your being and lose the illusionary self. That's all really. Life is happy to show us where a little self-reflection is still warranted. Be open to every experience just as Rumi welcomes each guest with open arms in his poem.

CONSCIOUSNESS
AND ESSENCE

The ego is nothing other than the focus of conscious attention.

Alan Watts

Paulo Coelho tells a beautiful story in which a young man wants to learn the secret of happiness. He goes to a wise man to ask him but he finds a crowded room in which many others want to talk to him. When after hours of waiting it was finally his turn to ask him for the secret of happiness, the wise man gave him a little exercise. "Take a stroll around the palace and come back after two hours." To make the task a little challenging, however, he put two drops of oil on a spoon and asked him to pay attention and not to spill it. The young man returned after two hours to the wise man with spoon in hand who had this to say:

> "So," asked the sage, "did you see the Persian tapestries hanging in my dining room? Did you see the garden that the Master of Gardeners took ten years to create? Did you notice the beautiful parchments in my library?" Embarrassed, the young man confessed that he had seen nothing. His only concern was not to spill the drops of oil that the wise man had entrusted to him. "So, go back and see the wonders of my world,"

*said the wise man. "You can't trust a man if you don't
know his house." Now more at ease, the young man
took the spoon and strolled again through the palace,
this time paying attention to all the works of art that
hung from the ceiling and walls. He saw the gardens,
the mountains all around the palace, the delicacy of
the flowers, the taste with which each work of art was
placed in its niche. Returning to the sage, he reported
in detail all that he had seen. "But where are the two
drops of oil that I entrusted to you?" asked the sage.
Looking down at the spoon, the young man realized
that he had spilled the oil. "Well, that is the only
advice I have to give you," said the sage of sages. "The
Secret of Happiness lies in looking at all the wonders
of the world and never forgetting the two drops of oil
in the spoon."*

The two drops of oil, by Paulo Coelho

A couple of interpretations of this insightful story come to mind.
The spoon with oil is what we focus on in life. We might crave
a promotion at work and step on other people's toes in order
to get it. If we somehow could just become aware of the bigger
picture we would realize that the perceived competitor is really
a friend who can help us in coming years. Our conscious focus
is as narrow as the spoon with two drops of oil, so we block out
a lot of information by narrowly zooming into our agenda. It is
said that we subconsciously have the ability to detect millions
of bits of information each second, while our conscious focus
only grasps about forty thousand bits. That is the meaning of
the spoon and the many treasures the young man missed out
on in his first round. Focus in the attempt to get something

from life comes at the expense of seeing the Oneness prevailing in life, and spiritual living invites us to see the whole instead of narrow parts and helps us enjoy the treasures few others seem to be able to see.

The second interpretation of the story is seemingly on the other side of the spectrum. In a spiritual quest, we go from narrow-minded self-focus to wanting to be spiritual which is also out of balance. When the young man went on the second round on the wise man's premises he spilled the oil altogether. In our attempts to be spiritual—loving, kind, forgiving, serene, without desire—we sell our authentic self short and burn the midnight oil so to speak. There is only bliss when the self merges in the magnificence of the now. The here and now always takes good care of our needs as well.

When the young apprentice went on his third round the balance was finally restored. We can admire life's treasures without negating what we are all about. Passion meets purpose, we love what we do and our tribe finds us. We create our idiosyncratic garden and are nourished by it. My friend David Wellens describes this Home-coming that is always at our disposal beautifully in this poem:

Our self
strives to
become

while

our SELF
rests in

BEING.

Are you expressing your essence?

Are you creating your garden?

Do you live your life authentically?

INVITE AWARENESS, PRACTICE SELF-AWARENESS

Ram said to Hanuman:
"What are you monkey?"
And Hanuman answered:
"When I don't know who I am, I serve You.
When I know who I Am, I Am You!"

Ram Dass

This is the religious version of the "I Am That Am" experience when the "I" melts into a higher dimension of Consciousness. The Zen-Buddhist version reads instead:

"When I don't know who I am, I am self-aware.
When I know who I Am, I Am Awareness."

It's a foolish errand to define the states that lie beyond the conscious grasp of the self-identity once it has taken a hold of us once again. Yet, we can be aware of these self-imposed limitations when the veil has dropped. Even if thanks to triggers, fears or our many aspirations we are temporarily completely unconscious. There always comes a time when we become conscious of this fact. So, in a sense we are always self-aware. Yet, being part of Awareness is an entirely different experience. "Breaking Free" outlines four attributes of being free in the pithy acronym S-E-L-F—Serenity, Energy, Love, and Flow. I wrote a poem, Rapture, to outline some signposts of these blissful states that we can sometimes get lost in:

> *God only knows how to drop the veil called*
> *self-identification,*
> *but some sounds herald the bliss of "I Am That*
> *I Am":*
>
> *There is the "ahh …", the pleasure of getting lost*
> *here now.*
> *There is that "pop"—the failure of a thought from*
> *forming.*
> *There is the "aha", the instance when mind grasps*
> *its agenda.*
> *There is the "snap", an energy link breaking for good.*
> *There is the silence, the stillness, and the serenity.*
> *And yes, there is the well-familiar, "yes, yes, yes".*
>
> Christian M. Wiese, Rapture

There is a big controversy in the spiritual community. Is there a process of self-transformation or is the magic of the here and now all that ever matters? Coaches will encourage you to make positive changes until you like the person you will one day become, whereas the enlightened voices will tell you that this "you" that you would like to transform doesn't exist. So, who is right? Perhaps both views have their merits? I am reminded of the wisdom of a rabbi who carried two pieces of paper in each trouser pocket, one reminding him that he is human just as everyone, the other encouraging him to reach for the stars. We are born with a limited body but have a mission to "be as Gods", as psychologist Erich Fromm once put it. The solution to the problem statement is simply, "I Am That I Am" never changes, but our self who is on a mission to receive Grace does. We have two eyes, so let's keep an eye on the human process of self-transformation as well as be open to the next moment of Grace where our self-identification ceases to exist.

The spiritual teacher J. Krishnamurti was once invited by a group of psychologists to discuss his philosophy with them. He reiterated in that setting that the inner revolution has to happen here and now or it never will. The psychologists reported that in their work people needed time for self-discovery and the healing of traumas. It was a frustrating exchange for all parties involved. I find this story a bit sad. Everyone in this room wanted to help people in distress, so why was it difficult to find some common ground? J. Krishnamurti was right to remind us that our mind can take the notion of self-improvement and self-transformation and put us on an endless treadmill. The opportunity to let go of all self and mind involvement is always here and now. Yet the psychologists are right in observing that letting go is often a process. We are human in the end.

I work with people who want to advance on their spiritual quest. I always perceive a change in their energy over time. Life changes us, a new job, a new love relationship, the loss of a loved one. The list of changes that life confronts us with is endless and we typically lose a piece of our self in the process. J. Krishnamurti himself, as a young man, was reported to have cried for 7 consecutive days when his beloved brother died. For me the expression enlightenment has two pieces to it. Like Moses experienced near the burning bush, the Light shines brightly with every "I Am That I Am" moment. Yet it is also true that with each spiritual break-through we tend to travel more lightly. Awakening is a steady letting go of self and life encourages us to let go all the time.

The spiritual evolution of self has four distinct stages, from self-identification to self-discovery and self-transformation to the blissful state that could temporarily be called as "cessation of self" altogether. We identify with our body, with our job and with our loved ones. We identify with our reputation, our belongings and our life story but then life happens and we get transformed by it. In this plane of consciousness, psychologists and spiritual life coaches have a similar mission to help their clients live a more fulfilled and happy life. It's the last stage, the dissolution of self, the "I Am That I Am" moment or Awareness—no process can get us there per se. Yet, life and our spiritual practices open us up for the next opportunity to leave the self behind.

Here is an example to illustrate the spiritual evolution of self. If a disillusioned businessman had come to me and asked me for a new way, a kinder and more loving environment of working with others, the inner revolution that I could point to is the self-centeredness within. With mindfulness, he could probably identify a craving for fame and recognition. Maybe that passion to succeed at any cost could be replaced with a new-found purpose, the appreciation and love to work with others, the meaning of creating something of value, the joy of sharing his wealth with those who are not as privileged as he is. These are some examples of self-discovery. "Why do I see my colleague as competition and not the missing piece of the puzzle?" "Why does it mean so much to me when people address me with a tone of reverence?" Self-transformation is when these insights set in, when we travel lighter after the weights of the past have been disposed. Yet, all these steps towards a more loving and meaningful world is not yet the cessation of self-identification altogether. So how exactly can we get there?

The Buddhist will say, **S**tillness does the job.

The kundalini energy yogi will tell you, it's all **E**nergy.

The Christians, and pretty much all religions will say, it's **L**ove,

and the Law of Attraction proponents will say it's all about the **F**low.

These are four different venues to pursue, and all of these approaches have their usefulness. S-E-L-F awaits us the moment we let go of s-e-l-f—selfishness, envy, loneliness and fear, and other less pleasant facets of our illusionary self. Just be still and feel the energy rising from within. Whenever you feel stuck, faced with life's problems, look out for the messages of synchronicity and love. The flow is always at hand once we open up to life again. Let's end this tug of war between the process of self-transformation and the power of now. We can be self-aware when we are once again as human as they come, and we can invite Awareness into our life moment by moment.

Opportunities for self-awareness

Letting go of the past
Being mindful of cravings and aversions
Acceptance of our self
Conflict resolution
Problem solving

Christian M. Wiese

Glimpses of Awareness

Follow the energy
Seeing Oneness in life
Feeling and expressing love
Creating a garden
Stillness and knowing

Grace finds us when we open up to life and are ready to lose our self. Outside of self-awareness and putting our best foot forward we do not have to do anything. Why should we chase what lies beyond our self? The higher Power that we look for is doing all the work for us. In Ramesh Balsekar's words:

If some Power has turned you into a seeker, don't you think it is the responsibility of that Power to take you where you are supposed to be taken?

Every living moment is an invite for Grace. Take a good look around. Do you see Her?

WHAT'S MISSING AT THIS MOMENT—CONNECT WITH S-E-L-F

We want to come to the present moment, to the realization that right now, this very instant, one is perfect. It's not a matter of trying to build up and improve one's self.

David Hoffmeister

Ramana Maharshi once asked during a lecture, "What's missing at this moment?" Everyone in the room was looking at each other smilingly. How right he was, the moment was just perfect. We should practice that inquiry more often. The ego seeks peace, seeks knowledge and searches for love. In Oneness, we carry peace in our heart. We know what we need to know at this moment. We are love and are surrounded by it. We can grasp the magnificence of the moment no matter whether it rains or shines.

The power of now, as Eckhard Tolle coined it, is available to us, not only in the presence of holy men like Ramana Maharshi but also in mundane moments, even at work. My friend Melissa Pope shared this observation as a caregiver of elderly:

> *Yesterday, while I was at my 93 year old client's home, I was grumbling within about*

> *something. Then I caught myself, "wanting to be elsewhere instead of the here and now that I was experiencing." As I reeled myself back to the present moment, I asked myself this question, "Are you really suffering in this present moment?" After I had asked myself this question, I observed my thoughts and feelings. I then answered my own question and said, "I am not suffering at all. Everything is actually quite fine." And then as I kept trying to spot any suffering at that moment, it actually brought me to a place of gratitude. I had so much to be grateful for at that moment. This little introspection turned everything around.*

You can try and see whether this "what's missing at the present moment" introspection helps you with your aches and pain. Often, we are telling each other mental stories that aren't even true. I remember how I carried stories around of how stressful my job was and if only I could follow my spiritual calling I would be healed. Well, guess what? After I stopped working in the financial industry I was telling myself the opposite story, namely how much I was missing the intellectual stimulus. When I realized the flip-flop in my story line I started laughing, "Looks like you are miserable no matter what!" There is a psychological entity at work that we can awaken from. It's like a bubble floating in our head that we can seemingly deflate with a mental needle and "puff", the story dissolves into nothingness. That's the power of now at our disposal.

Maybe I can leave you with this Awareness prayer that sums up the gist of this book perfectly:

*God, grant me the Awareness to experience Your
Grace, and give me the self-awareness to perceive
my self-imposed interferences, and the power to let
go of them.*

So, what's missing at this moment? Take a good look around right now and see for yourself. Chances are, S (erenity), E (nergy), L (ove), F (low) invites you to connect once again.

ALREADY FREE!

Freedom is not liberation in some heavenly world, but it is the freedom of every day, the freedom from jealousy, the freedom from attachment, the freedom from ambition, the freedom from competition, which is "the more", "I must be better", "I am this and must become that!"

J. Krishnamurti

"Buddhist therapist" Mark Epstein visited Ram Dass and told him about his work with his clients when Ram Dass replied, pretty much out of the blue, "Well, please remind them that they are already free!" Mark Epstein spent a few magical days in tropical Hawaii and felt this freedom. Alas, even before his return, his old world of conditioning and judgement caught up with him. While ordering lunch in a restaurant he was suddenly annoyed by the pickiness of Ram Dass' followers.

There was much commotion as a waitress began taking orders for Thai iced tea. A few people did not want ice; others could not drink condensed milk; many preferred theirs without sugar, and a few asked for splenda instead. Some people wanted hot tea while others wanted decaf. One woman asked the group to turn off their cell phones since their electromagnetic radiation worsened her arthritis. My judgmental thoughts, refreshingly absent during my watery sojourn, began to flow freely, and I was once again back to who I thought I was. Mark Epstein, Already Free, Essay

Mark's painful restaurant encounter after spending a beautiful few days with Ram Dass aptly describes the struggles many of us are facing. Moments of magic interchange with periods of being spiritually unconscious. It's alright! Just be one with the feelings that are running through you when you are off center. Just observe, without judging, without wishing the moment at hand away. Ram Dass' message to Mark Epstein is a curious one, "Please remind them that they are already free!" The question that arises is a spiritual quest about breaking free from our conditioning and our self-imposed limitations. Or are we in fact always free, and just temporarily forget our origin? This difference may sound semantic to you but it is quite important. This expression "breaking free" implies conscious work, an active quest, which naturally is part of a spiritual transformation. Yet, the expression "already free" reminds us that we don't have to do anything really. Be still, feel the love, see life's Oneness, and lose the imaginary self—just like that!

THE POWER OF S-E-L-F

This is the great mystery.
You do and do not exist.

Shen T'sing

I was sitting in morning contemplation stewing in anger over an issue that just refused to go away. Suddenly, I was engulfed in a cloud of unconditional love. I realized once again that our perspective is in fact upside down. Love and serenity is our true nature. It's the so-perceived problems and our reactions to them that are the clouds, covering Grace that is always at our disposal. That's the meaning of 'we are already free'. Problems come and go and some are self-inflicted as most of us are hardly saints. Yet, the higher dimension of being—Serenity, Energy, Love, Flow—is always at our grasp, for everyone. The power of S-E-L-F is a potent tool to help us snap out of whatever affliction that plagues us.

As within, so without! It's a big step forward into self-inquiry when we discover our own pain body is at work in the outside world. In the past we may have concluded, 'I hurt because ...'

- my colleagues undermine me.
- my problems (financial, health, accidents) are piling up.
- my partner doesn't love me anymore.
- my children are unruly.

With Awakening we still experience the outside disturbance, yet, we realize that the origin of the pain lies within and has to be addressed there just as much as it is necessary to face the problems in the outside world. Problems may have to be solved in time, but our attitude towards them can change in a heart-beat. We can withdraw our self-identification with it. Viewed from a higher plane of existence we stop shadow boxing. Why would I be mad at my colleague/partner/child if they just show me the inner work I have to face? I own this pain. I am responsible for it. I can let go of it. The solution to the problem is discovered within just as it is manifested in the outside world. I am empowerment, abundance, love!

When we practice self-inquiry it gets easier to access the power of S-E-L-F whenever we so choose. We get our arms around the interfering self-identification with the problem more easily and it becomes easier to let go and let the power of S-E-L-F do the magic. Let me give you a few personal examples in this direction.

Serenity

After living in the US for so long it was getting time for me to become a US citizen, but in order to keep my German passport as well, I had to apply for dual-citizenship at the consulate and was told that this process takes about a year. After 15 months I inquired what happened to my application and got a letter from Germany three days later informing me that they were still missing some information. Specifically, I had to prove that I still had ties to Germany. I got furious, mumbling to myself, "It took you 15 months to come up with this response! Keep your stupid passport!" Well, after a few minutes I calmed down and decided that this was just another step in the process. Of course, I have connections to Germany. My family lives there and for the longest time I covered Germany professionally. There are plenty of business-contacts as well. So, I sat down and wrote them a nice letter.

Isn't that how it goes with most problems? When we take our self-identification out of the picture and address the problem as it is, everything becomes much easier. It turned out that it was pure coincidence that after 15 months of processing my case the response from Germany had reached me in exactly the same week when I had inquired about it at the consulate. After sending my response, the application was quickly approved. That's the power of serenity at work. I am not saying that every problem gets resolved by having an open mind about it, but I am saying that solving a problem does get easier. Once again, every problem in our life is hand-delivered to perceive our self-identification at work and to transcend it. Serenity is a state that is always at our disposal.

Energy

I was playing golf with our youngest and given that we both have a competitive nature, we always play for pocket change. What a surprise to see him practicing breathing exercises whenever an important stroke came up. He gathered himself with an erect posture, breathing in and out rhythmically to calm his mind. He even mimicked the energy flow up and down his spine with his hand. I was amazed! I practice this breathing technique mentally all the time but to my knowledge have never demonstrated it in front of the boys. Well, good for him if he already knows the beneficial effects of prana yoga at the age of 14. When our energy flows freely, our thoughts stop and serenity prevails. This is a fact that you can discover for yourself.

As previously mentioned in the chapter on kundalini energy, only half of the survey respondents found the opening of our seven energy centers along the spine an important part of their awakening, although everyone experiences the inner energy flow. Spiritual living is having free-flowing heart-centered energy present with a still and open mind. Rhythmic breathing offers an instant opportunity to return to our center of being and to align the inner energies with the outer. In my experience, free-flowing kundalini energy also has proven health benefits and helps us greatly with our sleep patterns. Once all energy centers are open, extending all the way to the crown chakra, we naturally experience cosmic bliss.

Love

> *The Consciousness in you and the Consciousness in me, apparently two, really one, seek unity and that is love.*
>
> Nisargadatta Maharaj

Have you had a taste of free-flowing heart-centered energy completely outside of the conditioning of our mind? I got a glimpse of unconditional love when our boys were born. Though both are completely different, it is impossible to prefer one over the other. Love is unconditional! Romantic love is an equally strong energy link, but there is still a little subconscious possessiveness to make that what we admire in our partner our own. There is a little projecting and repressing when we put our rose-colored glasses on as we fall in love with the significant other.

Love is an energy connection, an entanglement with our aspirations personified by our significant other. Romantic love guides us on our path towards self-expression, self-discovery and self-transformation, so we have no choice but to follow our heart energy and life force. Time is the great villain or ally. We either lose interest in a person, or the mission we have signed up for, if we grow apart; or break through to unconditional love if we grow together. See your children grow up to become parents, spend your life with a partner or see your mission through until it develops a life on its own. Importantly though, time is not required at all. The opportunity to experience the clinging, projection and repression that keeps us from experiencing unconditional love is always here and now. Every moment we have gives us the chance to capture that essence in the other that is our own as well, divine Consciousness.

Love can be found everywhere. I had a break-through moment at work when I realized that someone I had once perceived as an adversary for years—until later signing up with him for a joint mission—was just like me. One fine day I was sitting opposite to him and realized, 'wait, he is me!' What a revelation! Oneness can be perceived in life's confusing dualities and when two come together, Consciousness can be recognized as one. Sometimes we discover the divine spark in each other. Sometimes we realize that our interaction merely mirrors back our own self-identification. Love is valuing our togetherness either way.

Flow

The flow is a vision, a feeling, a prevailing Oneness that we can perceive in any situation. I devoted my first two books, "The Magnificent Experiment" and "The Way of the Meister", to describing this non-dual harmony in life. What I find so fascinating about it is that we can experience this conflict-free state everywhere, even in places that we may not consider very spiritual. I had countless experiences of Oneness when I was at work. Consider this example: you take a colleague to a golf game, and just as you discuss some nasty internal company politics, you observe how your partner's golf bag keeps slamming into the back door of your car. You reduce the speed, take a deep breath and steer the conversation to more constructive solutions. Miraculously, the road becomes smoother as well. As you finally pull into the parking lot you both agree to mentor the new colleague who has a good chance at becoming the team leader. You stop the engine and observe that the time has just moved to 12:34, a sign of divine connection that is totally lost on your colleague. You smile and walk to your golf game.

The power of S-E-L-F is the truism that the inner state is mirrored in the outer world. Serenity and energy act on the inside. Love and flow capture the outside. You can start either way, the other is bound to follow. I awoke to the outside harmony of life and have been encouraged in my later years to seek within. Every Homecoming is different and you will find yours. We have so many different angles when it comes to self-inquiry and S-E-L-F expression, so pick the one that feels most natural to you in a given situation. Just remember that the opportunity to be free is here and now.

WE ARE WALKING EACH OTHER HOME!

A man was pretty good at his work,
but he realized deep down, he was sad.
To shake things up, he took a lunch stroll;
sometimes with colleagues, often by himself.
Nearby work there was a beautiful park.

One day in July he was lost in thoughts.
He walked through the park and perked up.
How could he have missed the wild rose?
He stood still and smelt the rose. Suddenly
he was "There", and knew he had always been.

I concluded my first book, "The Magnificent Experiment" with this park stroll experience and felt that it summed up the sudden slipping out of the "me, myself and I" energy rather well. Ten years later I would add the qualifier that we may have several of these break free experiences, and that we may still have some homework—a little misunderstood self-identification—to return to afterwards. I remember the story of a guru who had lost his son. He cried, and cried, and cried. Initially his disciples were very compassionate and understanding, but after a few days of continuous crying they lost their patience and said, "Master, you always told us this world is an illusion, then how come you are so devastated by the death of your son?"

The master replied, "Some illusions appear very real!", and kept wailing.

I work as a spiritual coach and have learned to be pragmatic. The self might not exist but if you are miserable and can't spot the serenity, energy, love & flow right now in your life, then working on your self might be the right medicine. Create that "story of me" that, temporarily at least, feels better. Your passion always leads you to your niche allowing you to express your unique energy signature. Time was created for a process to let go of "me energy" and sometimes we need it to ripen until the day when the fruit is ready to drop. Self-inquiry and self-awareness are both tools that help us discover the Awareness that is beyond as well as behind this "story of me". Eventually the truth of 'as within, so without' dawns on us, and that's when we have finally arrived at our destination. I consider myself a life artist. I have an eye for Oneness, the realization that we are mere actors in the game, the understanding that lover and beloved are one, just as much as I am the boss I would like to be, just as much as the colleague who competes with me for the spot. Everyone can perceive the prevailing Oneness. All conflict disappears when S-E-L-F is running the show. The inner is at peace, and the outer expresses the harmony that we experience within.

We don't exist on one plane of being, just as we are who we are on a different plane of existence. Sometimes we get the illusion, sometimes we don't. Some actors get so lost in the role that they temporarily forget that they are in a movie set. I have seen spiritual friends more powerful than me getting lost in misunderstood love, or in the role of a teacher. This gives me the confidence to tell you not to feel bad if you still experience a spiritual quest. Keep going, keep searching. You will find your answers as the perceived 'you' disintegrates. These concepts of separation are playing out in perceived time, and most of us are entangled in it in one form or the other. Yet, we have each other to break free together. We can enjoy the serenity, raise the energy vibration, feel the love and ride the flow. Life is magic when we open up to S-E-L-F. Every moment, we are invited to break free from the role we are playing. God is always nearby, and can always be best experienced via the tribe we have surrounded ourselves with.

I conclude this book with the awakening survey. I learned a lot from my spiritual friends over the years. The psychological processes that many of us experience—dark night of the soul, twin flame relationships, kundalini energy awakening, etc.— are often quite similar, yet, the idiosyncratic experience of Oneness is unique to our specific energy signature. Like in the story of the five blind men and the elephant, it helps to listen to each other's description of the indescribable, and to embark on the mission together to remove these self-induced shackles. My salute goes out not only to those who walk with me, but also to those who have launched me on this spiritual quest in perceived conflict. They taught me so much about my self-imposed illusions. I value them just as much as my trusted guides who show me what it means to be free. Everyone is God speaking, so everyone should be appreciated even if we temporarily turn in different directions.

Never mind if you enjoy the power of S-E-L-F but a friend comes along and pulls you right back into the illusion. Taking a step back after we have advanced by two is part of the foundation building. Every occurrence serves a divine purpose. We still have a little work to do on this blue planet and the next entanglement just means we have another priceless opportunity for self inquiry and S-E-L-F expression. Let's keep learning together. Let's keep walking together.

We are all going to the same place, and we are all on a path. Sometimes our paths converge. Sometimes they separate, and we can hardly see each other, much less hear each other. But on the good days, we're walking on the same path, close together, and we are walking each other Home.
Ram Dass

APPENDIX

I conducted a survey where I asked 41 long standing spiritual friends for their awakening experiences. Twenty-six women participated and 15 men. Most of the respondents are in their 40s and 50s, with a few in their 30s and in their 60s and 70s. Most reported that they had been on an awakening quest of 10 years and more.

There was no "scientific" selection of the participants. Many of these friends crossed my path over the course of my 12-year awakening journey and left a mark one way or another. I consider these friends my peers. Some have been mentees or clients at some stage, but each of them moved along their own path. In my experience, there is no hierarchy when it comes to spirituality. Some folks have been at it a little longer. Some are temporarily a bit more in tune with Oneness than others. Some have already found what they set out to find while others are still searching. Yet, we are all the same, or as one survey participant put what she saw it in her vision, *"We are like snowflakes uniquely different on one level, yet all the same as another."* Anyone who sets out on a quest for a world beyond the "me, myself and I" qualifies as a participant of this awakening survey.

Question 1: Describe your current state:

  a. Spiritually curious
  b. Awakening—On a quest that is beyond myself
  c. The journey is finished—I am blessed with purpose and peace of mind—I am centered in the Self
  d. All of the above—a little bit of everything
  e. None of the above. These answers don't resonate/don't make sense.

Apparently, everyone had moved passed the simple curiosity stage. Out of 4 remaining responses, answers were split fairly evenly between "Awakening" (14) and "A little bit of everything" (14); 7 respondents felt the quest had come to an end for them, while 6 participants couldn't resonate with the offered categories. One friend explained his "none of the above" answer in the following way:

I am not on a spiritual journey and never have been, even though some fourteen years ago I would have said I was on a journey and a hardcore seeker. Ultimately, everything is spiritual so if you single one thing out over another (what we all tend to do) you will "search forever and never find." In other words, that which is always present (not lost) cannot be found.

"Breaking Free" is written for you, as you hold this book in your hands, it is meaningful to you. Even my friend had to admit that 14 years prior he perceived a quest as well. So what if the perspective changes once we have reached the imaginary mountain top and discover that we are already free and as a matter of fact always have been. The status of our quest moves from the desire to break free to the realization that we already are. My friend and I argued back and forth on this point for a long time without getting anywhere, yet he did admit the other day in a conversation that he was impressed by my ability as a coach to jump into the trenches so to speak and accompany the seeker in her quest. He added that he just can't do it anymore. The energy is just not there. I can understand that. Perhaps that will be me one day too. Each to their own!

Question 2: Was there an awakening moment that launched you on your path?

Only very few respondents fell into the traditional enlightenment category in which they described the "I" perception disappearing from one day to the next. For most, awakening is a series of "cracking open" events as one respondent described this experience so well. Twenty-three out of 41 participants remembered one particular event that towered over everything else. The catalysts of awakening are numerous; illness, drugs, passing of a loved one, divorce, addiction, lost twin love, guidance of a guru, discovery of metaphysical talents, near death experience, dramatic revelation, satori moment, and kundalini awakening.

One respondent put her awakening experience in the following way: *"The floor actually seemed to fall out underneath me, landing exactly where I had always been but with no perception that there was a separate me doing it."*

One respondent experienced a vision of Oneness involving food: *"I saw a hamburger, and was shown how it is filled in different countries, even a German one. I got it, there is one base, the core, and different religions add to it. There is only one God.*

Boom, after this thought I was filled with such peace, light, it's beyond words. I just knew that it was our Divine Home. It lasted only a short while.

One respondent had a major spiritual breakthrough during a near death experience as a child. In her words, *"The Angels have been with me since and have been guiding me in my choices. I was 3 years old when this happened but not until my teens did I become fully aware that no one I ever met saw what I saw. So, I thought for a while that something was wrong with me and I became silent."*

One woman had a major awakening breakthrough around the passing of a loved one. *"My greatest healing revelation came about 20 years ago. I was talking to a close friend on the phone. At the time, his wife and my friend as well were near death and we were supporting each other. At the moment of her transition we both felt her presence and out of nowhere I had a revelation and a profound clarity that "I" was not this person. At that moment all guilt, shame, feelings of failure and every conscious belief vanished from my mind."*

One participant was catapulted to new heights of Consciousness with the help of a guru. In her words, *"I visited Sai Baba's ashram, spending 4 months with him. I quickly experienced complete and inner renunciation."* One participant had a major breakthrough moment while acting. In his words, *"I lost myself in a character far from the role I had been playing my entire life. This fragility scared me and for years I questioned what I felt."*

Another friend's awakening journey started when he was smoking marijuana: *"I thought I was going to die, but it was my awakening and now nothing can stop me."*

And as already mentioned, awakening can happen with soul wrenching losses as well. *"I have always been very connected with my Angelic team and Spirit. However, a lifetime of living with fearful abusive humans assisted in shutting a lot down. When my dad committed suicide in 2011 was a huge cracking open moment. I began to reconnect with spirits of those who had left form very intensely at his time. I also went through another big Ascension launch in 2012 when I finally gathered up the courage to leave my painful and abusive 20-year marriage."*

One respondent experienced a revelation while working his shift. *"After having been involved in a Christian cult for 35 years which is now in the process of imploding, my path led me to A Course in Miracles. Soon thereafter while still driving a San Diego city bus, I was commissioned by a dramatic revelation."*

The remaining group of people (9) experienced awakening as a series of transformative events. In contrast, 5 respondents perceived no awakening event or process at all. "I was born awake", one voice said. "I was born with a deep peace and mindfulness", another friend added. So, while the majority experience; awakening as a breaking free of self, some conclude that we are already born free.

Question 3: Did your Awakening journey coincide with a healing journey?

a. No
b. Yes, please share

The overwhelming majority (32) reported awakening as a healing journey, while 9 respondents did not. A couple of respondents felt strongly that you cannot have awakening without healing: "The awakening journey cannot be anything else but a healing journey. We learn that the ego is an illusion." Still, for a small number of respondents the spiritual breakthrough didn't coincide with healing. Among the rest, the recovery answers varied. Lots of trauma was reported that needed to be worked off, as well as addiction, diseases and near-death experiences.

Question 4: Do you have a spiritual "talent"
(Empath, Psychic, Medium, etc.)

    a. No
    b. Yes, please share

The majority of respondents reported having talents that are hard for the scientific folks to get their arms around. Ten people, in contrast, felt that they had no special talent. A couple of respondents pointed out that the expression "talent" was misplaced given that they were born with these abilities. "I am an empath", one friend responded, "and I was born that way." Anyway, the list of these special abilities is impressive and would fill pages. For illustrative purposes, I again share a few quotes below. There was in fact a time when I researched these phenomena. I wanted to know for sure whether there is a metaphysical world beyond our scientific understanding of reality. Now that many of these mystical occurrences have happened to me or to my friends in my presence, I no longer feel that we have to prove anything. Rather, Oneness is a reality that anyone with a spiritual mindset and eyes to see can perceive.

Almost everyone in the survey professes to be an empath. As one woman put it, "*I feel everything 100 percent or more, the good, the bad, and the ugly. I am too easily drained by negative people. When you love, you really love and when you break, you are really broken.*" Several men claimed that their empathic abilities made them quite outgoing, "*I always say the right thing at the right time.*" "*I always bump into people I know, or that are ready to connect with me.*" "*I can have conversations with people and make them calm and feel easy.*"

A few participants claimed that everyone has access to these metaphysical abilities. One woman described her abilities in the following way: "*There was not one singular definite awakening experience for me. I was born awake to more than my "singular" self and perpetually throughout my life have experienced mediumship, multi-dimensionality, lucid dreaming, visions, clairvoyance, clairaudience, empathic and healing abilities, and a connection to God, the Source, Jesus, and so forth. I cannot describe as "talents" more that these abilities are natural and inherent within Consciousness, as part of the expanded individuated experience that everyone has the capacity for at some point. The "spiritualized ego" loves to weave an inflated identity through our attachment to such phenomena.*"

Mediumship is the ability to connect with departed beings. One other woman claimed that this ability is ever-present for anyone bold enough to reach out to this energy. "*I am a psychic medium but I will never say that it is a talent or a gift because it is a natural use of our senses open to anyone. The only thing is one has to let go of conditioning and beliefs about it and have no fear.*"

A number of survey participants professed to be clairsentient, clairvoyant, and clairaudient. My phone conversation with the woman from the UK who could feel what was going on in my body was a great example in this direction. Several clairvoyants in our survey see the future in dreams or visions. One woman gave the following example of what it means to be clairaudient, she said she was getting ready for work on a Saturday and heard the word "traffic" loud and clear. Later that day she was caught in traffic wherever she went whereas traffic ran smoothly in the opposite direction.

This group also had many healers, Reiki masters, tarot readers and one sorcerer. Several women professed that they can see the auras of people. A number of women from Northern Europe reported the ability to see and communicate with nature spirits, one woman replied she feels the living energies of special trees, and a couple of respondents experienced past-life regressions.

Question 5: Are you a light worker? (Raise humanity, help humanity, spread the light?)

    a. No
    b. Yes; in what function?

Twenty-two respondents classified themselves as light workers, 8 answered maybe or said that they at least tried. Eleven couldn't resonate with this expression and said "no". This group of people has many professions and callings in which we have the opportunity to make people's days, such as caretaker of the elderly, therapist, social worker, author, minister, coach, teacher, fisherman, chef, activist, healer, physical therapist, Reiki practitioner, doctor, medium, psychic, and many others. All of them can bring a lot of "good" and light to the people they work with the help of their many spiritual talents.

Question 6: Do you consider yourself devout?

   a. No

   b. Yes, what holy Institution do you appeal to?

Just as was the case with the somewhat opaque expression light worker in question 5, most respondents struggled with the religious association of the word "devout". We only had two respondents who were devout practitioners of Christianity and Islam. The majority of respondents answered "no", yet 20 respondents felt devoted to more spiritual concepts instead (guru, nature, Oneness, God, all faiths, life, love, universe, healing, light).

Question 7 What is your favorite "centering" activity (meditation, yoga, art, music, prayer, etc.)?

All survey participants recognized the need to stay centered. Just like in question 4 though when I asked for the "talents", the responses ranged all over the place. I list them below in no particular order:

Meditation, affirmation, mantra, music, prayer, talking to Guides, chanting, singing, composing, poetry, writing, painting, art, dancing and silence.

Yoga, crystals, tai chi, martial arts, love making, conscious breathing, swimming, showering, nature, being with animals, gardening, earthing, life, folding laundry, woodwork, healthy eating, cooking, sun bathing, having spiritual conversations, alone time, people, spiritual lectures, mindfulness (witnessing thoughts), lying flat on the ground.

BIBLIOGRAPHY

Joseph Benner, The Impersonal Life

Evelyn Blau, Krishnamurti, 100 Years

Paulo Coelho, The Alchemist

Ram Dass, Be Here Now

Mark Epstein, M.D., Open to Desire

Debbie Ford, The Dark Side of the Light Chasers

Erich Fromm, You Shall Be as Gods

Bruce Hood, The Self Illusion—How the Social Brain Creates Identity

Kim-Anne Jannes, Das Ich als Lehrer des Lebens—Vom gesunden Umgang mit dem Ego

William James, The Varieties of Religious Experience

Jack Kornfield, A Path with Heart

Jiddu Krishnamurti, On God

Suzhen Liu, Letting Go—Release Your Suffering

Gerald G. May, M.D., Will and Spirit

Gabor Mate, In the Realm of Hungry Ghosts

Swami Nikhilananda, The Gospel of Sri Ramakrishna

James Redfield, The Celestine Prophecy

Helen Schucman, A Course in Miracles

Daniel J. Siegel, The Mindful Brain

Vivekananda, Raja Yoga

Christian M. Wiese, The Magnificent Experiment—The Magic of Connecting with Your Tao

Christian M. Wiese, The Way of the Meister

Printed in the United States
by Baker & Taylor Publisher Services